making
pillows
& slipcovers

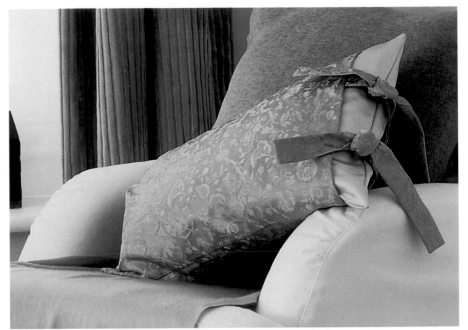

making
pillows
& slipcovers

cushions, bolsters, bean bags, and chair covers to transform your home

dorothy wood

southwater

This edition is published by Southwater

Southwater is an imprint of
Anness Publishing Limited
Hermes House
88–89 Blackfriars Road
London
SE1 8HA
tel. 020 7401 2077
fax 020 7633 9499

Distributed in the UK by
The Manning Partnership
251–253 London Road East
Batheaston
Bath BA1 7RL
tel. 01225 852 727
fax 01225 852 852

Distributed in the USA by
Anness Publishing Inc.
27 West 20th Street
Suite 504
New York
NY 10011
fax 212 807 6813

Distributed in Australia by
Sandstone Publishing
Unit 1, 360 Norton Street
Leichhardt
New South Wales
tel. 02 9560 7888
fax 02 9560 7488

10 9 8 7 6 5 4 3 2 1

Publisher **Joanna Lorenz**
Managing Editor **Judith Simons**
Project Editor **Simona Hill**
Photographer **Paul Bricknell**
Step-by-step Photographer **Rodney Forte**
Stylist **Juliana Leite Goad**
Designer **Lisa Tai**
Editorial Reader **Kate Sillence**
Production Controller **Don Campaniello**

Previously published as part of a larger compendium, *The Practical Encyclopedia of Soft Furnishings*.

contents

introduction

There is an abundance of beautiful fabrics that can be made into cushions and loose covers to transform a room, adding a splash of colour to contrast with, or match your decor. Whatever your style, from plain piped cushions to shaped loose covers, there are ideas to suit all tastes.

cushions

Cushions are the accessories in a decor theme and as such add the finishing touch to a room. They can be made in almost any fabric and are one of the most creative aspects of soft furnishing. Cushions in contrasting colours enliven an otherwise flat colour scheme, and are the perfect opportunity to add an accent colour to a room. They add warmth and comfort to a sofa or armchair, and soften the hard edges of furniture. A single scatter (throw) cushion or bolster can inspire the entire interior scheme for a room, or cushions can be carefully chosen at the end to complete the decorating process with touches of colour and textures of fabrics you may not have had the opportunity to use.

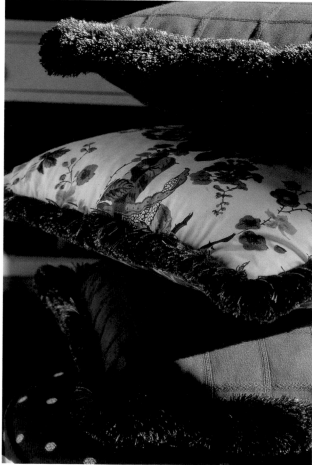

above left Cushions can be made in almost any fabric and in any shape and can be finished with a variety of complementary trims and decorative buttons.

below left A wonderfully plush fringing can transform beautiful fabrics into something quite exotic and luxurious.

above Scatter (throw) cushions and a bolster piled on top of a large footstool make a comfortable day bed. The different-shaped cushions are made from an assortment of fabrics and the co-ordinating colour scheme links them all together.

Cushions come in practically any shape or size and can be used in any room in the house. Because there is such a myriad of styles, cushions are one of the most creative aspects of soft furnishing. It is possible to use almost any fabric for a cushion if it is purely decorative and so you can really let your imagination run riot.

Scatter (throw) cushions are versatile – they can be tossed on to a bed, piled on the floor or propped in the corner of an armchair to add a little extra comfort. It is better to make them fairly large if you want to group them, as lots of little cushions can look rather cluttered.

Cushions are the easiest item of soft furnishing to make and the complete novice can tackle the simpler styles. In this chapter there are lots of different styles to choose from and different methods of inserting the cushion pad. Which you choose is often personal preference but each style

of cushion cover has been made with the easiest and most suitable method. The openings can also be decorative – a row of buttons down one edge, some pretty ribbon ties or, for an unusual nautical look, cord laced through eyelets.

You can also add a touch of individuality with some unusual trimmings, making the variations on the basic scatter cushion almost endless. It is not only the edges of the cushions that can be decorative; the large area on the front of the cushion cover is the ideal shape for some beautiful handiwork. Simple machine-embroidered motifs repeated over the surface often look most effective, or a larger design can be embroidered using crewel work, Mountmellick embroidery or cross stitch. Fabric crafts such as patchwork and appliqué are also suitable. These techniques can be used to make the cushions as modern or traditional as you like.

The majority of cushions may be square or rectangular but cushion pads are available in an amazing assortment of shapes and sizes, including circles and hearts. Square cushions range from the small 30cm/ 12in size to the extra-large 55cm/22in which is suitable for a Japanese-style floor cushion. There is plenty of choice in rectangular pads too. Some are almost square and others very long and thin. If you can't find the shape you are looking for, it is quite easy to make your own pad using foam chips, polyester stuffing or feathers. The most expensive filling is feathers, but it lasts much longer than other types and does not go lumpy or flat. The casing on a feather cushion pad should be made from heavyweight

above left Large-scale cushions always look substantial and make a chair more appealing.

above Small motifs, stitched in a contrasting thread, make an Oxford cushion special. Keeping the border area stitch-free gives the cushions a fuss-free look.

left All sorts of fabrics can be used to make cushions. This windowseat cushion has been made from linen dish towels. The tie quilting helps to hold the feather stuffing in position and adds a subtle finishing touch.

calico that helps prevent the ends of the feathers from escaping.

Box-style cushions are similar to scatter (throw) cushions but they have a gusset running around the edge. Feather-filled, box-style cushion pads are available but you can also use a specially cut piece of foam instead. These cushions are ideal for softening a wicker chair or wooden bench or they can be made in extra-large sizes for seating in a child's bedroom or as a bed for a pet. The most suitable filling for larger floor cushions is polyester bead filling, obtainable from most haberdashery stores. The fabrics used for this style of cushion are generally more practical as the cover will need to be removed for cleaning. Even so there are lots of possibilities, from crisp linen or cotton ticking to warm fleece fabrics.

Bolster cushions add an elegant touch, tucked into the arm of a sofa or used as a day pillow on a couch or chaise longue. Depending on how they are going to be used, bolsters can be purely practical or highly decorative. At its most basic, a bolster cushion cover is simply a long tube tied at either end of the cushion pad. This may sound rather plain, but when it is made in crushed organza, the result is a stunningly stylish cushion. More formal bolster cushion covers have a classic piped edge, and covered buttons or luxurious tassels at each end.

above Crisp blue-and-white canvas cushions trimmed with eyelets and white cord create a distinctive nautical look.
left A variety of checked and striped fabrics work well together in co-ordinating colours. Some of the striped fabrics have been joined diagonally to make unusual cushion panels.

basic cushion with a zipper

A zipper is a practical fastener for a cushion cover. Depending on the shape and size of the cushion, it can be placed in a seam, partway down the back, or in the centre of the back. Concealing a zipper in a seam makes sense, but is only suitable if the seam is straight. Zippers are best placed along the bottom edge of a square cushion, or in a side seam on a rectangular cushion. Choose a strong dressweight zipper that matches the fabric colour; a shade darker will be less visible than a lighter one. To add interest to a basic cushion, use different fabrics for the front and back or insert a contrast panel.

you will need

- **paper and pencil for template**
- **cushion pad**
- **fabric A, for the cushion front**
- **fabric B, for the cushion front**
- **fabric C, for the cushion back**
- **dressweight zipper**
- **sewing kit**

tip for basic cushion with a zipper
Buy a zipper 5–10cm/2–4in shorter than the side seam.

1 Draw a paper template the same size as the cushion pad and fold it in three. Use the folded template to cut out the front panels, adding a 1.5cm/⅝in seam allowance all around. Unfold the template and cut out a cushion back. With right sides together, pin and stitch each front panel to the next along the long edge. Press the seams away from the lightest colour fabric.

2 With right sides together, pin the front and back together down one short side. Centre the zipper on the side seam and mark the position. Stitch up to the marks at each end. Reinforce the stitching by working a reverse stitch at the zipper tab end. Tack (baste) the seam together between the stitches.

3 Press the seam open. Place the cushion cover right side down on a flat surface. Pin the zipper right side down along the tacked seam.

4 Tack along the zipper tape on both sides of the zipper, then mark each end of the zipper teeth with tacking stitches. Working from the right side and using a zipper foot, stitch just inside the tacking stitches, close to the zipper. Pull out the tacking threads and open the zipper slightly. Fold the cushion cover in half, with right sides together, and pin the other seams. Stitch each in place using a 1.5cm/⅝in seam. Trim across the corners and turn through. Ease out the corners from the right side, press, and insert the cushion pad.

basic cushion with a concealed zipper

If a square or rectangular cushion has any attachments such as tassels, braid or cord that could get caught in the zipper teeth, it is better to fit the zipper on the back panel and the braids around the front panel.

you will need

- **paper and pencil for template**
- **cushion pad**
- **fabric A, for the cushion front**
- **fabric B, for the cushion back**
- **dressweight zipper**
- **4 tassels, 5–8cm/2–3in long**
- **sewing kit**

tips for basic cushion with a
concealed zipper
When using bold patterned fabric, match the
pattern along the seam lines of the back panels.

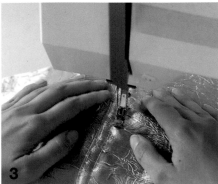

1 Cut out a cushion front the same size as the cushion pad plus 1.5cm/⅝in seam allowance all around. Draw a paper pattern the same size as the cushion pad and mark a line from side to side about one-quarter of the way down. Cut the pattern along the line. Cut out two fabric pieces for each side of the cushion back, adding 1.5cm/⅝in seam allowance all around. Press under 1cm/½in along the top long edge of the large panel and 2cm/¾in along the long lower edge of the smaller panel. Zigzag-stitch the raw edges.

2 With the zipper tab on the right-hand side, pin the pressed edge of the large panel along the bottom of the zipper teeth, then tack (baste) and machine stitch in place.

3 Pin the small panel over the zipper so that it overlaps the other panel by 3mm/⅛in. Working from the right side, tack the other side of the zipper. Using a zipper foot attachment, stitch the zipper.

4 Pin a tassel to each corner of the front cover before stitching the front and back together. Alternatively, thread the tassel cord into a large-eyed needle and insert it into the finished cover from the right side.

basic cushion with a semi-concealed zipper

This method of inserting a zipper is used when the cushion is circular or an unusual shape. The zipper is inserted, either horizontally or vertically, across the widest part of the cushion back, depending upon the cushion shape, and in a place where it will be less conspicuous.

you will need

- **paper and pencil for template**
- **round cushion pad**
- **fabric, for the cushion front and back**
- **dressweight zipper**
- **fringing**
- **sewing kit**

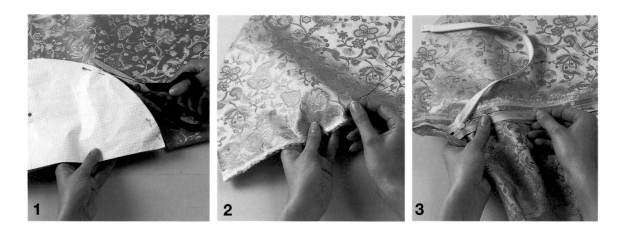

tips for basic cushion with a semi-concealed zipper
- To calculate the length of fringing on a circular cushion multiply the diameter by 3.14.
- Zigzag-stitch close to the stitching to finish raw edges and trim the excess fabric.

1 Draw a paper template the same size as the cushion pad adding 1.5cm/⅝in all round. Cut one cushion front. Fold and cut the template in half across the centre line. Use one piece to cut out two back panels, adding 1.5cm/⅝in seam allowance to the straight edge.

2 Centre the zipper along the straight edge of one back panel and mark its position. Remove the zipper. Place the two halves of the cushion back right sides together.

3 Stitch the seam at each end up to the marks. Tack (baste) the section of seam inbetween the stitching and then press the seam open. With the zipper open and right side down, align the teeth with the seam, and pin in place. Tack along one side of the zipper, 3mm/⅛in from the teeth. Close the zipper, then pin and tack the other side, again 3mm/⅛in from the teeth.

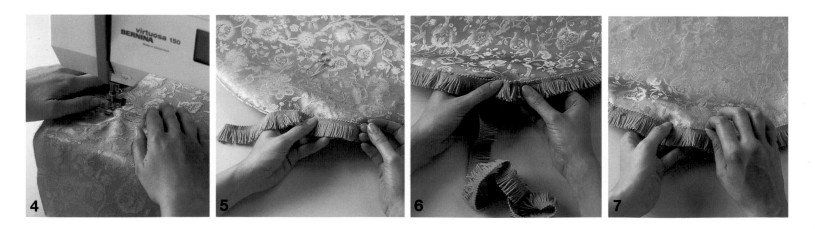

4 Stitch the zipper from the right side. At the corner, count the number of stitches into the centre and stitch the same number on both sides to make sure they are equal. Pin and stitch the front cover to the back.

5 Beginning in the middle of the bottom edge, pin the fringe or braid around the cushion cover. Tack (baste) in place.

6 Trim the ends so that they overlap slightly, then neatly fold under the ends so that they meet, and slip-stitch the join.

7 Oversew or back stitch the braid to the front of the cover, without catching the underside in the stitching. Match the thread to the braid and use the least conspicuous stitch.

piping a cushion

Piping adds a professional finish to a cushion and emphasizes its shape, particularly if the piping is in a contrasting colour to the main body of the cushion. Piping cord is available in a range of thicknesses and the piping fabric can be in a contrasting or matching fabric type to the cushion. Choose the thickness of cord according to the size of the cushion and the effect required.

you will need

- **cushion pad**
- **one cushion front**
- **one made-up cushion back**
- **5mm/¼ in wide piping cord**
- **dressweight zipper (optional)**
- **bias strips (see basic techniques)**
- **sewing kit**

tip for piping a cushion

Join the ends of the piping in the centre of the bottom edge of the cushion using one of the methods described in the basic techniques chapter.

1 Cut a cushion front and make a cushion back, adding a zipper if desired. Cut bias strips wide enough to fold over the piping cord leaving a 1.5cm/⅝in seam allowance. Pin the bias strips around the cord and stitch close to the cord, using a zipper foot attachment.

2 Pin and tack (baste) the piping around the edge of the cushion front with raw edges facing outwards. Snip into the seam allowance to allow the piping to bend around the corners.

3 If using a zipper, open it slightly. With right sides together, pin the front and back covers together. If the fabric is slippery, such as velvet, tack them together first. Stitch as close as possible to the piping cord, using a zipper foot attachment. Trim the corners and turn through.

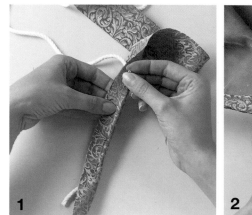

1

2

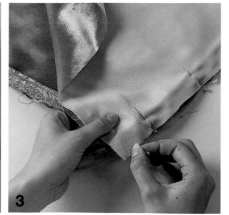

3

frilled cushion

A frill gives a cushion a pretty, feminine look. It can be made from matching fabric or a contrast such as lace or ribbon. To find the length of frill required for a circular cushion, measure around the outside edge of the cushion pad and then double the length. For a square or rectangular cushion, allow four times the length plus four times the depth.

you will need

- **cushion pad**
- **one cushion front**
- **one made-up cushion back**
- **fabric, for the frill**
- **sewing kit**

tip for frilled cushion

Add piping around the edge of the front panel before pinning the frill in place.

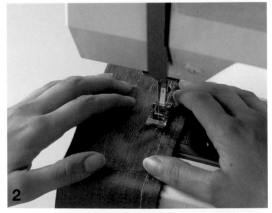

1 Cut a cushion front and make a cushion back, adding a zipper or envelope opening as desired. Decide on the width of the frill, usually about 8cm/3in. Cut sufficient strips of fabric to fit around the cushion, twice this width, plus 3cm/1¼in seam allowance. Join the strips together at the short ends into a continuous loop with plain seams. Press the seams open and trim to 5mm/¼in.

2 Fold the frill in half widthways, right side out and raw edges aligned. Sew a row of gathering stitches at each side of the seamline, using a long machine stitch. Start a new thread at each join rather than stitching all the way around.

3 Fold the frill into four. Mark the cushion cover into quarters. Pin the frill to the cover, aligning the folds and marks, then pull up the gathers evenly. Adjust, allowing slightly more fullness at the corners. Tack (baste) in position and stitch.

basic cushion with a back envelope opening

An envelope opening is a good alternative to a zipper. If the two hems overlap by less than 10cm/4in, a fastening such as buttons or poppers (snaps) will be needed to hold the edges together.

you will need

- **paper and pencil for the template**
- **cushion pad**
- **fabric, for the cushion front and back**
- **sewing kit**

tip for basic cushion with a back envelope opening

Reverse stitch along the side seams where the hems overlap for extra strength.

1 Draw a paper template the same size as the cushion pad and cut it in half widthways. For the cushion back, cut out one panel this size and a second panel about 15cm/6in longer, adding 1.5cm/⅝in seam allowance all around each side. Press under a 2cm/¾in hem on each panel where they will overlap and stitch. Cut out a full-size piece of fabric for the front cover, adding 1.5cm/⅝in seam allowance all around.

2 Place the front cover right side up. Pin the back panels to the front along the top and bottom edges with right sides together. Overlap the hems, keeping the larger panel on top and pin in place.

3 Stitch the front and back together using a 1.5cm/⅝in seam allowance. Trim across the corners and turn through.

above *Envelope openings are an easy alternative to inserting zippers and a good first project.*

basic cushion with a front envelope opening

An overlap makes an attractive feature on the front of a cushion. It can be horizontal or vertical. For a centre opening, plan the overlap so that the buttons are positioned in the centre of the cushion.

you will need

- **fabric, for the buttons**
- **button kit**
- **cushion pad**
- **fabric, for the cushion front and back**
- **sewing kit**

tip for basic cushion with a front envelope opening
If the overlap is off-centre make sure the size of the panels are in proportion to the finished cushion.

1 Decide what size buttons you wish to use and how many are needed to fit across the cushion pad. Cover the buttons with a contrast fabric, using a button kit (see basic techniques).

2 For the two halves of the cushion front, cut a piece of fabric 30cm/12in wider than the cushion pad, adding 3cm/1¼in seam allowance to the width. Cut the fabric in half widthways, then measure an 8cm/3in turning on each cut edge and fold under to the wrong side. Cut the fabric for the back cover, allowing 1.5cm/⅝in seam allowance all around.

3 Allowing for the seams, space the buttons right side down along the folded edge of one panel. Position the buttons at least half the width of the button away from the fold and insert pins to mark the length of the buttonholes, allowing an extra 3mm/⅛in ease. Stitch the buttonholes and cut between the stitching.

4 Overlap the two front panels so that the buttonhole side is on top. With right sides together, pin the back cover on top and trim any excess fabric from each end. Stitch, reverse stitching where the panels overlap for extra strength. Turn through to the right side. Mark the position of the buttons and sew in place.

1

2

3

Oxford cushion

A classic Oxford cushion has a plain flat flange around the edge of the cushion pad. The flange is a flat fabric border created by cutting the cushion cover extra large and stitching a line around the edge before inserting the cushion pad.

you will need

- **paper and pencil for the template**
- **cushion pad**
- **fabric, for the cushion front and back**
- **sewing kit**

tips for Oxford cushion

- Use a piece of masking tape to mark the width of the flange on the needle plate before beginning to stitch.
- The size of the flange should be in proportion to the size of the pad. A 5cm/2in flange is ideal for a 40cm/16in pad.
- A basic back envelope opening is the neatest method for this type of cushion.

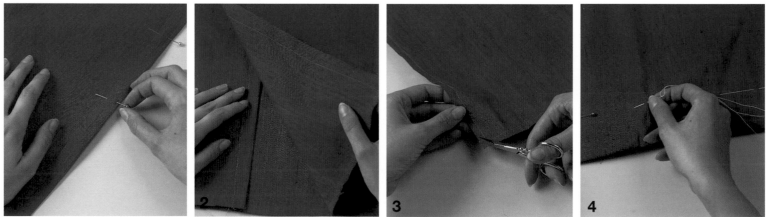

1 Measure the cushion pad and add the flange width all around. Draw a paper template adding 1.5cm/⅝in seam allowance and cut out a piece of fabric to this size for the front cover. Cut the template in half widthways and cut out one back panel this size. Cut out another back panel 15cm/6in longer. Press under or pin a 2cm/¾in hem on each panel where they will overlap. Stitch.

2 With rights sides together, pin the back panels along the top and bottom edges to the cushion front. Overlap the hems, keeping the larger panel on top.

3 Stitch the front and back together with a 1cm/½in seam, reverse stitching along the side seams where the hems overlap for extra strength. Trim across the corners to reduce bulk.

4 Turn the cushion cover through to the right side, ease out the corners carefully and press. Pin and tack (baste) around the cover 5cm/2in from the stitched edge. Stitch just inside the tacked line. Remove the tacking threads and insert the cushion pad.

padding an Oxford cushion

Padding the cushion edge gives a softer finish to an Oxford cushion. The flange is usually narrower than on a standard Oxford cushion and can be padded with thick wadding (batting) to look like heavy piping.

you will need

- **cushion pad**
- **one cushion front**
- **one made-up cushion back (see Oxford cushion)**
- **25g/1oz wadding (batting)**
- **sewing kit**

tip for padding an Oxford cushion
Use a zipper foot attachment to stitch close to the padded edge.

1 Make the cushion cover in the same way as an Oxford cushion. Before turning the cushion cover through to the right side, mark the size of the cushion pad in the centre of the cover. Mark the position with pins.

2 Cut strips of wadding (batting) to fit between the pins and the stitching. They should be 3–5mm/⅛–¼in narrower, depending on the thickness of the wadding.

3 Pin the wadding around the edge of the cushion cover, trimming to fit at the corners. Tack (baste) the wadding in place, taking care to stitch through just one layer of fabric.

4 Turn the cushion cover through and ease out the corners. Pin and then tack just inside the edge of the wadding. Stitch.

tied cushion

This pretty cushion cover is rather like a pillowcase, with an opening on one side that is fastened with ties. The ties can be made with a square or angled length and as narrow or wide as you would like. The cushion pad is visible inside the tie opening and should be covered with a contrasting fabric.

you will need

- **cushion pad**
- **fabric A, for the inner casing**
- **fabric B, for the outer casing and ties**
- **sewing kit**

tip for tied cushion

The length of the ties depends on whether you want to tie a bow or a simple knot, so tie a strip of fabric to decide the ideal length.

1 Measure the cushion pad and make the inner casing (see basic cushion with a back envelope opening). For the front and back outer casing, add 3cm/1¼in for seam allowances to the width and 20cm/8in to the length. Cut two pieces of fabric to these measurements. Stitch the long sides and one short side. Trim the seams and the corners.

2 Cut four ties twice the width required plus 3cm/1¼in seam allowance. Fold each tie in half widthways with right sides together. Stitch across the top and down the long side. Trim across the corners and turn through.

3 Cut 17cm/6½in off the length of the cushion casing, cutting from the unstitched end, and reserve for the facing. Turn the cover through to the right side and press. With raw edges together, pin the ties on top, securing two to each side and making sure they match and are evenly spaced. Tack (baste) them securely in place.

4 Turn under a narrow 5mm/¼in hem along one edge of the facing and stitch. Match the seams carefully. With right sides together and raw edges aligned, pin the facing to the cushion cover, trapping the ties. Stitch in place 1.5cm/⅝in from the edge.

5 To get a neat opening edge, press the seam flat between the facing and the cushion cover, then fold the facing to the inside and press the edge from the reverse side.

6 Stitch around the opening, 4cm/1½in from the folded edge to secure the facing. Use the lines on the needle plate or attach a piece of masking tape for accuracy. Press.

mitred border cushion

A mitred border is a neat, attractive way to frame an unusual piece of fabric or appliqué, or an embroidered panel. The cushion can have a zipper along the seam line joining the back to the front or an envelope opening at the back. To plan the mitres, draw a template the exact size of the cushion pad and mark the inset panel.

you will need

- **cushion pad**
- **fabric A, for the centre panel**
- **fabric B, for the mitred border**
- **one made-up cushion back**
- **sewing kit**

tip for mitred border cushion
Mark the size of the inset panel in tracing paper so that you can centre a motif before cutting out.

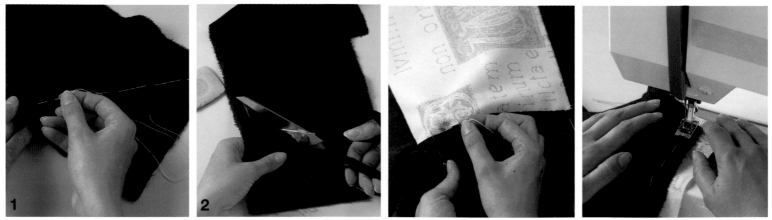

1 To make the mitred frame, cut four strips of fabric the length of the cushion pad plus 1.5cm/⅝in seam allowance on all sides. Place two strips right sides together, and fold back a corner 45°. Open out and tack (baste) along the foldline.

2 Stitch the two pieces together along the tacked line, beginning stitching 1.5cm/⅝in from the inside edge. Trim the seam to 5mm/¼in and press open. Join on the other strips in the same way to make a square frame.

3 Press under 1.5cm/⅝in seam allowance on the inside edge of the frame. Centre the inset panel on the reverse side and pin in place, with right sides together. Slip-tack the panel in place from the right side.

4 Folding back one side at a time, stitch the sides of the inset panel to the mitred border. Stop stitching at the seam of each mitre. Remove the tacking threads and press. Attach the cushion back.

flap cushion

A flap is a simple way to make an opening in a cushion cover. It can be held in place with a sash or with a fastening such as buttons, ties or poppers (snaps). The depth of the flap depends on the shape of the cushion as it has to be sufficient to lie flat, but it is usually at least one-third of the depth of the front panel. On a narrow, rectangular cushion the flap can come halfway down the front of the cushion.

you will need

- **paper and pencil for the template**
- **one cushion pad**
- **fabric A, for the cushion front and facing**
- **fabric B, for the cushion back and flap**
- **fabric C, for the tie**
- **25g/1oz wadding (batting)**
- **sewing kit**

tip for flap cushion

Cut a strip of scrap fabric and tie around the cushion pad to find the length required for the sash.

1 Draw a paper template the same size as the cushion pad, adding the flap to the top edge. Cut out a back cover and a facing to the size of the template, adding 1.5cm/⅝in seam allowance all round. Pin the facing and back cover right sides together and mark the depth of the flap plus the seam allowance, at each side with tailor's chalk.

2 Stitch the two pieces together between the marks, reverse stitching at each end of the flap for strength. Snip into the seam allowance at each side, trim across the corners and turn through.

3 Cut out the front panel to the size of the template minus the flap, adding 10cm/4in for the facing. Turn under 5mm/¼in along the facing edge and stitch. With right sides together, pin the front panel to the back cover. Turn over the facing at the top of the front panel and pin in line with the flap as shown.

4 Stitch around the remaining three sides, reverse stitching at each end for strength. Zigzag-stitch the seam allowance and trim neatly.

5 Cut two pieces of fabric long enough to fit around the cushion and tie at the front. Cut the ends at 45°. Cut a piece of thin wadding (batting) the same size and pin to one side. Stitch, leaving a gap for turning.

6 Trim the wadding close to the stitching and trim across the corners to reduce bulk. Turn the sash through and press lightly. Slip-stitch the gap. Tie the sash around the finished cushion.

heart-shaped cushion pad

Small, shaped cushions add interest rather than comfort to a group of scatter (throw) cushions. If you make the pad yourself the cushion can be any simple shape that you like. Stuff the pad with feathers, polyester stuffing or foam chips.

you will need

- **paper and pencil for the template**
- **calico**
- **stuffing**
- **sewing kit**

tip for heart-shaped cushion pad
Use a "featherproof" weight of calico to prevent feathers escaping from the cushion pad.

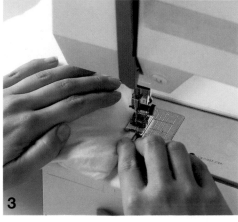

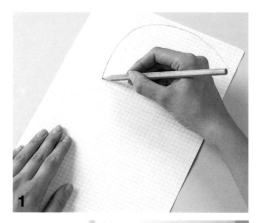

1 Draw the desired cushion shape on paper. Use this as a template to cut out two pieces of calico, including 1.5cm/⅝in seam allowance all round. Tack (baste) the two pieces together.

2 Stitch around the edge, leaving a gap along one of the straighter edges. If you are making a heart shape, snip into the "V" at the top and notch the curves. Turn through and stuff firmly with your chosen filling.

3 Pin the gap closed and stitch the edges together by machine, or slip-stitch the opening shut.

heart-shaped cushion cover

Making a shaped cushion cover is not difficult, especially if you have made the cushion pad yourself. It is actually very easy to make the pad, and that way you will be confident that the cover you make will be exactly the right shape and size.

you will need

- **paper and pencil to make the template**
- **velvet**
- **sewing kit**

tip for heart-shaped cushion cover

If the cushion is quite large insert a zipper or make an envelope opening in the back across the widest part of the cover.

1 Draw round the cushion pad to make a paper template. Cut out two pieces to this size for the front and back covers, adding 1.5cm/⅝in seam allowance all round.

2 With right sides together, tack (baste) the two pieces together. Tacking is particularly important when using velvet as the fabric has a tendency to creep (move).

3 Stitch, leaving a large gap for inserting the cushion pad along one straighter side. Snip into the "V" at the top of the heart and along any inward-facing curves. Cut notches around the outward-facing curves, making the notches closer together on deeper curves. Trim across the point of the heart.

4 Turn the cushion cover through and insert the pad. Pin the gap closed and slip-stitch securely.

round box cushion

Box cushions have a gusset separating the front and back panel. The cushion pads, which can be bought in similar shapes and sizes to ordinary pads, also have a gusset. Box cushions usually have a zipper opening in the centre of the gusset along the back edge.

you will need

- paper and pencil to make a template
- round box cushion pad
- fabric
- dressweight zipper
- two covered buttons (see basic techniques)

tip for round box cushion

When adding the buttons, pull together firmly to make an indent on the flat sides of the cushion.

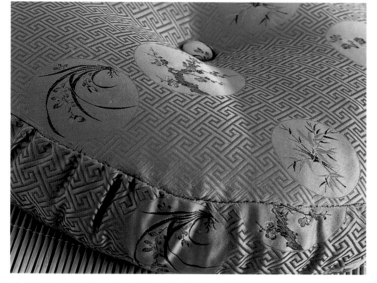

above *Tied buttons keep the cushion in a flat shape.*

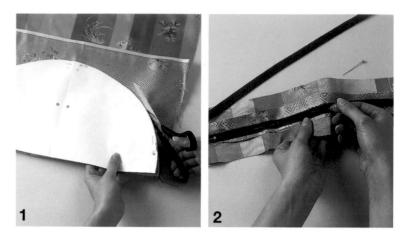

1 Measure the cushion pad to make a paper template. Cut out the template, adding 1.5cm/⅝in seam allowance all round. Cut one front and one back cover using the template. Measure the depth of the cushion pad. Cut out one piece of fabric the depth of the pad plus 6cm/2½in for seam allowances, and the length of the zipper, plus seam allowances.

2 To make the zipper panel, cut the strip of fabric in half lengthways. Place the pieces right sides together and tack (baste) along one long edge. Open out. Mark the length of the zipper in the centre and stitch the seam allowance at each end. Press the seam open and centre the zipper teeth on the tacked line. Pin in place, then tack down each side 3mm/⅛in from the zipper teeth. Stitch just outside the tacking stitches from the right side.

3 Cut out the rest of the gusset, adding 1.5cm/⅝in seam allowance all round. With right sides together, stitch one end of the gusset to the zipper panel and press the seams open. Pin in place around the front cover.

4 Pin the other end of the gusset to the zipper panel. Remove several pins and stitch the gusset ends together. Open the zipper. Pin the back cover in place.

5 Stitch the cushion back and front in place. Notch the curves. Turn the cushion cover through and insert the cushion pad.

6 Mark the centre front and back with pins. Using strong thread and a long needle, thread a button on to one side. Push the needle right through the pad. Thread on the other button on the other side. Fasten off the thread securely.

square box cushion with piped sides

Piping defines the edges of a box cushion and is particularly effective in a contrast colour. For an unusual effect, back muslin with a contrasting firm fabric.

above *Backing the lightweight muslin with calico stabilizes the finished project.*

you will need

- square cushion pad
- backing fabric
- muslin
- contrast fabric for piping
- piping cord
- dressweight zipper
- sewing kit

tip for square box cushion with piped sides
Before fitting the back cover, snip into the gusset at each corner to ensure that it is absolutely square.

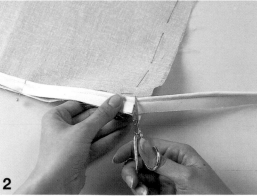

right *These box cushions have been made without piping.*

1 Cut a back and front cover the size of the cushion pad plus 1.5cm/⅝in seam allowance all round. Cut the same from muslin. With wrong sides together, steam press each muslin piece to each backing piece. Tack (baste) the layers together around the edge.

2 Make up the required length of piping (see basic techniques). Pin the piping along the edge of the right side of the front and back covers. Snip into the raw edges of the piping at the corners. Join the ends and stitch in place using a zipper foot attachment.

3 Cut a gusset to fit around three sides of the pad. Fit a zipper into the remaining side and make the gusset into a continuous strip. With right sides together, tack the gusset in place between the front and back. Stitch close to the piping and turn through.

bolster cushion with gathered ends

Bolster cushions are an ideal armrest or headrest for a sqfa or bed. Add a tassel or button at each end of the bolster to finish the ends.

To calculate the amount of fabric needed for a bolster, measure the length and circumference of the bolster pad. The length of fabric for the gathered ends is the circumference of the pad and the width is equal to the radius. The cover needs an opening wide enough for the bolster pad to be inserted along the side seam, so fit a zipper, or alternatively slip-stitch the gap once the pad is in place.

above *Buttons or tassels add a decorative finish.*

you will need
- **bolster cushion**
- **main fabric**
- **contrast fabric**
- **piping cord**
- **button kit**
- **zipper (optional)**
- **sewing kit**

tip for bolster cushion with gathered ends
Trim the piping cord flush with the seam to reduce bulk.

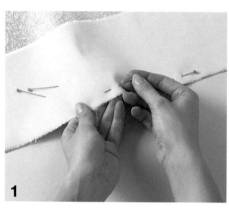

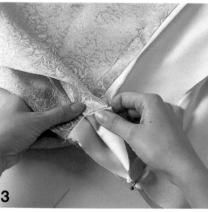

1 Measure the length and circumference of the bolster pad and make a pattern. Cut 13cm/5in from each end. Use the centre panel to cut the main fabric, and the end panels to cut the contrast, adding 1.5cm/⅝in seam allowance to all sides. With right sides together, pin and stitch the borders to the main panel.

2 With the main fabric, make piping to fit along each short end of the bolster (see basic techniques). Pin and tack (baste) in place with raw edges aligned.

3 For the gathered ends, cut out two lengths of contrast fabric, the length of the bolster's circumference and as wide as the radius, plus 1.5cm/⅝in seam allowance. Stitch in place, sandwiching the piping. Matching the seams, stitch the side seam, leaving a gap. Insert a zipper if desired. Press.

4 Stitch two rows of gathering threads around each end of the bolster. Pull up the threads tightly.

5 Holding each gathered end in turn, wrap a strong thread around just below the gathers. Fasten off securely. Turn the bolster cover through the side opening.

6 Cover two large buttons, using a button kit. Thread them into the centre of the gathers, one at each end of the bolster, then stitch the thread ends in securely. Insert the bolster pad and slip-stitch the gap if you do not have a zipper.

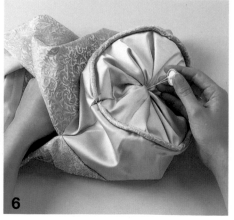

flat-end bolster cushion

This bolster cover has plain instead of gathered ends, with piping to define the shape. Using contrast fabric for the ends creates an elegant effect.

you will need

- **bolster cushion pad**
- **paper and pencil to make a template**
- **main fabric**
- **contrast fabric**
- **piping cord**
- **dressweight zipper (optional)**
- **sewing kit**

tips for flat-end bolster cushion

- When stitching a circle, work at a slow speed and feed the fabric at a slight angle to create a smooth curve.
- Join the ends of the piping by stitching a seam and trimming the piping cord so that it runs right round the circle.

1 Draw a paper template to fit the end of the bolster pad and add a 1.5cm/⅝in seam allowance all around. Using contrast fabric cut out two circles.

2 Measure a length of piping cord to fit around the bolster ends. Cover in the main fabric (see basic techniques). With raw edges aligned, pin the piping around the edge of each contrast circle. Join the ends neatly and stitch using a zipper foot.

3 Cut out the main panel to fit the bolster pad, adding 1.5cm/⅝in seam allowance all round. With right sides together, pin the long edges. Mark the position of the gap for inserting the pad or the zipper, and stitch from the marked point to the edge of the fabric. Add a zipper if required.

4 With right sides together, pin the circular ends to the main panel. Stitch in place close to the piping, using a zipper foot.

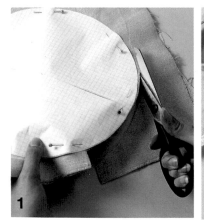

1

2

3

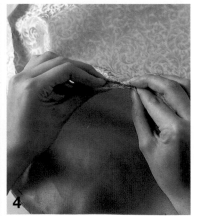

4

tied-end bolster cushion

This is the easiest style of bolster cover to make and is particularly effective as a pillow on a day bed or sofa. A rich fabric such as crushed metallic organza adds a touch of luxury to the simple design.

you will need

- **bolster cushion pad**
- **metallic organza or lightweight fabric**
- **sewing kit**

tip for tied-end bolster cushion

Because the seam may be visible inside the tie ends, a French seam is used to enclose the raw edges neatly.

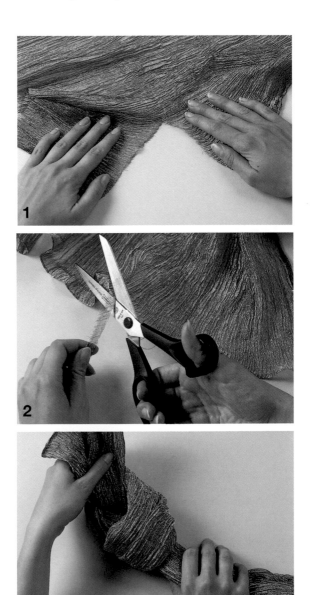

1 Measure the length and circumference of the bolster pad. Add 50cm/20in to each end for the ties and 1.5cm/⅝in seam allowance to the circumference. Pull a thread or tear carefully across the width of the fabric to straighten it before cutting, as shown.

2 Turn under 1cm/⅜in along the edge of the fabric at each short end and stitch, stretching the fabric slightly as you go. Trim the seam allowance close to the stitching.

Fold the stitched edge over to make a narrow hem at each end and stitch again on top of the previous stitching. Fold the fabric in half length-ways, wrong sides together to make a tube, and stitch a 7mm/⅜in seam. Trim the seam to 5mm/¼in and press open. Turn the tube through to enclose the raw edges and stitch a second 7mm/⅜in seam. Turn right side out.

3 Tie the fabric in a knot at one end. Insert the bolster pad and tie the other end.

flat cushion with ties

A beautifully tailored cushion will transform a hard wooden chair, making it more comfortable and much warmer to sit on. Use a fabric to match curtains or other cushions already in the room. Add fabric or ribbon ties to hold it securely in position.

you will need

- **paper and pencil to make a template**
- **main fabric**
- **contrast fabric**
- **blunt tool**
- **wadding (batting)**
- **sewing kit**

tip for flat cushion with ties

Cut a strip of fabric and tie around the chair back to find the exact length of tie required.

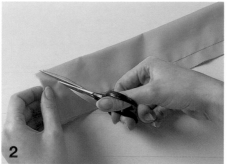

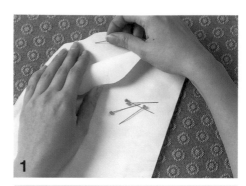

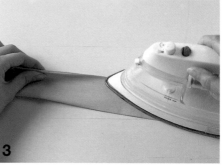

above *Ties can be as plain or flamboyant as you like.*

1 Make a paper template of the chair seat, carefully marking the position of the back of the seat for the ties. Fold in half. Place the fold along the centre of the fabric design, if any, and pin. Open out the template and cut out two full-size fabric pieces, adding 1.5cm/⅝in seam allowance all round.

2 Cut four strips of contrast fabric, each 8 x 50cm/3 x 20in. With right sides together, fold each in half lengthways. Stitch down the long side and diagonally across one short end to create a neat finish for the end of the tie. Trim the excess fabric from the pointed end to reduce bulk.

3 Turn the ties through and ease out the point with a blunt tool. Roll the seam between your thumb and finger, then press.

4 With raw edges aligned, pin two ties to each back corner of a cushion piece, on the right side. Bundle the tie ends in the centre.

5 Place a second cushion piece on top of the first, with right sides together, then add a piece of wadding (batting) cut to size on top. Pin the layers together then stitch around the edge, leaving a gap along the back for turning through.

6 Notch the outward-facing curves and turn through. Ease out the seams and pin all the way around. Slip-stitch the gap.

7 Using a slightly longer stitch, top-stitch around the cushion 1.5cm/⅝in from the stitched edge. Mark the lines with a fabric marker if you are unsure. Tie the pad in position on the chair back.

frilled stool or chair cushion

A frill is a very pretty way to finish a cushion. The main difference between a stool and a chair cushion is the positioning of the ties. On a stool, the ties are attached underneath the frill so that they can be tied around the legs. A chair cushion has no frill along the back and the back ties are attached to the end of the frill at both corners.

you will need
- paper and pencil for a template
- main fabric
- 100g/4oz wadding (batting)
- contrast fabric for frill and ties
- sewing kit

tip for frilled stool or chair cushion
Fold the frill on to the reverse side of the cushion and leave for a day or two to "set" the frill so that it will hang neatly.

1 Draw a paper template of the stool seat, marking the position of the legs. Cut out two pieces of the main fabric, adding 1.5 cm /⅝in seam allowance. Cut two layers of 100g/4oz wadding (batting) to the same size. Measure round one of the pieces to find the circumference of the cushion.

2 Decide on the depth of the frill and cut strips twice this measurement, plus 3cm/1¼in seam allowance. The frill length is twice the circumference of the cushion. With right sides together, stitch the lengths together to make a circle. Fold in half lengthways, with wrong sides together. Fold the frill into four equal pieces and press the folds. Stitch two rows of gathering stitches between the folds.

3 Tie off one end of each set of gathering threads. Fold the top cover piece in four and mark the quarter sections. Pin the frill to each section matching the folds to the quarter sections, then gently pull the gathers up to fit. Distribute the gathers evenly then pin the frill and cover together. Tack (baste) the gathers and remove the pins. Stitch in place.

4 For each tie, cut one strip of fabric 8cm x 1m/3in x 1yd. Fold each in half lengthways, right sides together. Stitch around the raw edges, leaving a gap in the centre. Trim the seams and across the corners. Turn through and slip-stitch the gap. Fold in half and pin the fold to the cover in the position of each stool leg. Bundle the ends in the centre. Place the bottom cover on top with right sides together, then two layers of wadding, and pin. Stitch, leaving a gap for turning. Notch round the curved edge, turn through and slip-stitch the gap. Press the frill.

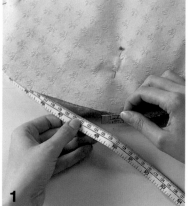

1

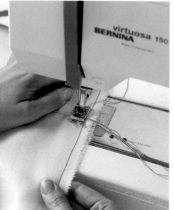

2

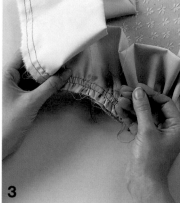

3

4

box-style shaped cushion

Some chairs are more comfortable with the addition of a thick, fitted cushion. Make a template of the shape required, then have the cushion pad cut to shape from foam. Stitch a layer of wadding (batting) to the foam.

you will need

- **paper and pencil to make a template**
- **main fabric**
- **foam, cut to size, for the pad**
- **dressweight zipper**
- **piping cord**
- **sewing kit**

tip for box-style shaped cushion

For added softness, cover the foam with a layer of wadding before covering.

1 To make a template, tuck a large sheet of paper into the chair, folding in the edges until it is the exact size, then trim to fit. Cut out two pieces of fabric to this size, adding 1.5cm/⅝in seam allowance all round. Measure the curved area to find the optimum zipper length.

2 Cut out the gusset for the straight side the depth of the cushion pad plus the seam allowance. Cut the gusset for the curved zipper edge 3cm/1¼in wider, then cut in half lengthways and tack (baste) together. Mark the length of the zipper and stitch the seam at each end. Tack, then stitch the zipper in place. Stitch the main gusset to the zipper gusset.

3 Make two lengths of piping to fit around the cushion pad (see basic techniques). Beginning at the centre back, pin the piping around the edge, snipping the piping at the corners. Overlap the ends and trim the cord back to the seamline. Tack in place.

4 With right sides together, pin the gusset around the cushion pad, with the zipper along the curved edge. Stitch in position. Open the zipper slightly. Pin the other side of the cover in place. Stitch and turn through. Fold the pad in half to insert it into the cover.

1

2

3

4

fleece pet bed

Fleece is the ideal fabric for a pet's bed as it doesn't crease and can be washed easily. The size of the bed will depend on the size of your pet. This bed is 70cm/28in diameter and 15cm/6in deep.

you will need

- **paper and pencil to make a template**
- **calico for lining**
- **fleece fur fabric**
- **upholstery zipper**
- **washable polyester stuffing or polystyrene beads (styrofoam pellets)**
- **sewing kit**

tips for fleece pet bed

- The zipper has to be as long as possible so that the liner can be inserted easily. Buy zipper tape by the metre, long enough to fit halfway round the gusset.
- See basic techniques for instructions to insert the zipper.

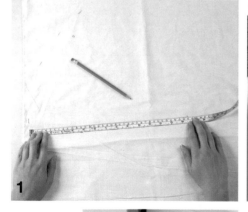

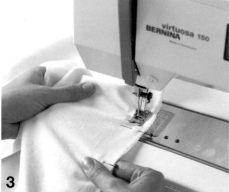

1 Draw a circle the required size of the base on to calico. Cut two pieces for the lining plus seam allowances. Cut the same from main fabric. Measure around the circle to find the length of the gusset and add seam allowances. Cut one piece from calico and one from the fabric 18cm/7in wide.

2 From the main fabric gusset piece, cut a length 5cm/2in longer than the zipper. Cut in half lengthways then tack (baste) along one long edge, with right sides together, 1.5cm/⅝in from the raw edge. Stitch in the zipper, then pull out the tacking threads.

3 Pin and stitch the zipper panel to the rest of the gusset. With right sides together, pin the gusset to the top circle of fabric, easing in the fabric to fit. Stitch in place with a 1.5cm/⅝in seam. Open the zipper slightly. Stitch the bottom circle in position in the same way then turn the bed through. Make up the calico liner in the same way, but leaving a large gap for stuffing instead of the zipper.

4 Stuff the liner with washable polyester stuffing or polystyrene beads (sytrofoam pellets) until it is fairly firm. Pin and stitch the gap, reverse stitching for extra security. Insert the liner into the cover.

shaped beanbag

Beanbags are fun for children and make ideal seating in their bedrooms. They are easy to move around as they are so light, and this one can be hung up out of the way using the handle at the top. These measurements will make a small beanbag for a toddler or young child, and could be scaled up to adult size. Make the liner from a soft, loose-weave calico that will stretch to take the shape of the body.

you will need

- calico for lining
- paper and pencil to make a template
- fleece fabric
- polystyrene beads (styrofoam pellets)
- sewing kit

tip for shaped beanbag

Only fill the liner half full of polystyrene beads so that they have plenty of room to move about when you sit down.

1 2 3 4

1 For the side lining, cut a piece of calico, 70 x 150cm/28 x 59in. Draw a line across the width 30cm/12in from one long end. The bag top shaping begins at this point. Use the pattern at the back of the book as a guide to shape the sides . Place the marked calico on top of the fleece and cut out both together, adding 1.5cm/⅝in seam allowance on the shaped sections. Separate the lining from the fleece.

2 With right sides together, stitch the straight back seam. Pin adjacent diagonal edges together and stitch. At the point, take the last few stitches along the edge of the fold and tie off the threads securely. Repeat for the calico lining.

3 For the base, cut a 50cm/20in diameter circle from calico and fold in half. Using the half circle as a template, cut two half pieces from fleece, adding a seam allowance to the straight side. Insert a zipper between the straight edges.

4 To make a handle, cut one piece of fleece 20 x 6cm/8 x 2½in. Fold in half lengthways, with right sides together and stitch the long edge. Turn right side out and centre the seam in the middle back and top stitch. To make the bag top, cut an 18cm/7in diameter circle from fleece and calico. Position the handle on the right side, trim the raw edges and pin in place. With right sides together, pin the bag top and bottom to the sides of the beanbag. Open the zipper slightly before stitching each in place all the way round. Turn the bag right side out. Make up the liner in the same way, but instead of adding a zipper to the base, use the calico base template whole and leave a large gap in the seam joining it to the bag sides. Half-fill the liner with polystyrene beads (styrofoam pellets), then stitch the gap securely. Insert the liner into the cover.

chair covers

Slipcovers are made to protect favourite upholstery, to hide faded or damaged furniture, or to completely alter its appearance. When you put a slipcover on a chair or footstool, you have the opportunity to transform a piece of furniture, adding ties, tabs and buttons as desired. Choose colours that complement your room scheme either by introducing new accent colours as a contrast or choosing solid colours that enhance existing furnishings. Slipcovers are the ideal way to freshen up a dull or dated interior scheme and can be used to ring the changes, so that the appearance of a room changes with the seasons – cool, crisp linen for summer and warm, rich colours for winter.

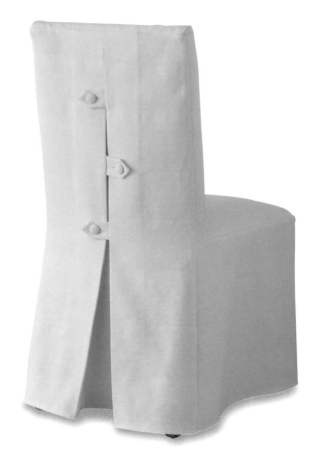

Slipcovers are literally clothes for furniture and as such can change the appearance of chairs, footstools or ottomans dramatically. Just like clothes, a slipcover can be casual or classic, plain or exotic depending on the style and fabric chosen. Unlike the majority of clothes, slipcovers cannot be bought off the shelf or even made to a pattern because there are so many different shapes. Each cover has to be designed individually and fitted to the particular piece of furniture. Obviously some styles of furniture are easier to cover than others but, as a general rule, a tight-fitting cover is more difficult to cut and fit than a looser style.

Don't be too adventurous to begin with – choose a footstool or an odd chair as a first project that you would like to match to other furniture in a room. Look at magazines and catalogues for inspiration and pick out features that you like, such as hemlines, trimmings or fabric, bearing in mind that the new cover should blend into its new surroundings.

There are lots of different fabrics that you can use for soft furnishings, but slipcovers should be made from a proper furnishing fabric. These fabrics are sold in wider widths than dress fabrics and are harder-wearing. They are often fire-retardant to set standards and can be washed or dry-cleaned. It is essential to pre-shrink fabric before making it up into slip covers, otherwise you may not get it back on after cleaning.

This chapter has design ideas for covering a variety of different chairs and footstools. It is unlikely that your furniture will look the same, but by reading and understanding the step-by-step instructions on pin-fitting and cutting fabrics you should be able to make a tailor-made cover for your piece of furniture.

above left Simple tabs and covered buttons make an effective and attractive fastening down the back of this dining chair cover.

above Square-shaped chairs suit slip covers with flat valances and neat inverted box pleats at each corner.

right Pretty self-coloured fabric bows soften the lines of this fully fitted dining chair cover and give it a less formal look.

left Spaced box pleats use much less fabric than traditional full pleats, and add a more textural finish to the bottom edge of an armchair or sofa cover.

far left Careful use of piping makes the matching of stripes or checks on a slipcover less of a problem.

making a pattern for a dining chair

Dining chairs come in all shapes and sizes, but any of them can be fitted with a slipcover. The cover may be to protect the chair, to hide a chair that has seen better days or to make your dining room look more formal. The first thing is to create a pattern, and the easiest way to do this is by "pin-fitting" a cheap fabric such as calico or curtain lining, which will follow the shape of the chair. The pattern can then be used to cut out and make one or several slipcovers.

Each chair is different, so you need to decide the style you want to create. Is the opening to be a zipper hidden in one of the seams, or do you want a more decorative opening down the back? Do you want to cover the legs, or does the chair have elegant Queen Anne feet that you wish to show? As you begin to pin-fit, it will become obvious how the fabric is going to lie and whether darts are needed for shaping. If the chair has a shaped back, a gusset will almost certainly be required to follow the curve. The advantage of using a cheap fabric for pin-fitting is that mistakes can be made and rectified before you cut the main fabric.

you will need
- **calico**
- **pencil**
- **sewing kit**

right *If you are making just one slipcover, the pattern could be used as a lining for the main fabric.*

1 Begin with a piece of calico at least 8cm/3in larger all round than the area you want to cover. Fit the front of the chair back first, aligning the straight grain of the fabric with the centre line of the chair. Work out from the centre to the outside edges, inserting pins every 5–8cm/2–3in, and pulling the fabric to fit snugly.

2 Once you are satisfied with the fit of the calico, trim the excess fabric, leaving approximately 2.5cm/1in seam allowance along the side edges, and the bottom edge, if you have chosen to fit the seat and chair back as two separate pieces.

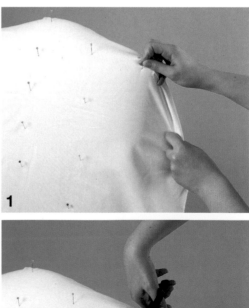

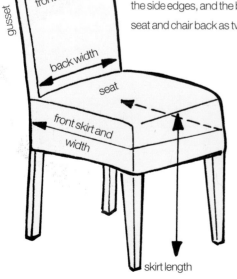

left *Each dining chair is slightly different, but the terminology used is the same. The skirt length doesn't necessarily reach the floor.*

gusset
front chair back
back width
seat
front skirt and width
skirt length

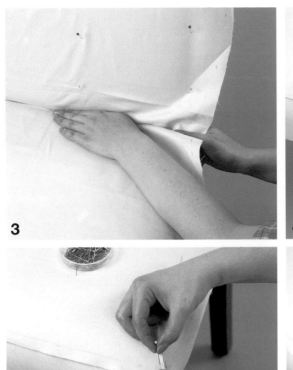

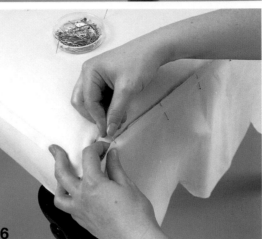

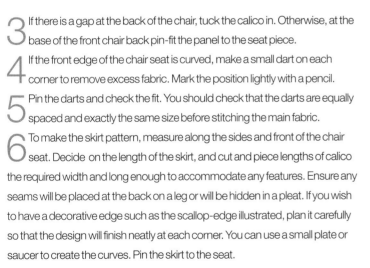

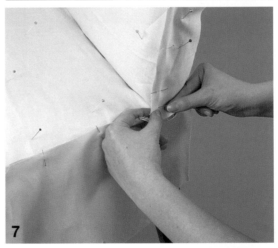

3 If there is a gap at the back of the chair, tuck the calico in. Otherwise, at the base of the front chair back pin-fit the panel to the seat piece.

4 If the front edge of the chair seat is curved, make a small dart on each corner to remove excess fabric. Mark the position lightly with a pencil.

5 Pin the darts and check the fit. You should check that the darts are equally spaced and exactly the same size before stitching the main fabric.

6 To make the skirt pattern, measure along the sides and front of the chair seat. Decide on the length of the skirt, and cut and piece lengths of calico the required width and long enough to accommodate any features. Ensure any seams will be placed at the back on a leg or will be hidden in a pleat. If you wish to have a decorative edge such as the scallop-edge illustrated, plan it carefully so that the design will finish neatly at each corner. You can use a small plate or saucer to create the curves. Pin the skirt to the seat.

7 If the chair back is quite thick, you will need a gusset panel to join the inside and outside chair back panels together. Measure the width of the gusset (the thickness of the chair back) and add 2.5cm/1in seam allowance. The gusset may be narrower at the top. Cut a strip of calico this width and pin to the chair front. Pin the seams, attaching the gusset to the top edge of the skirt. Repeat at the other side of the chair.

8 Fit another strip along the top edge of the chair (it may be possible to make the entire gusset from one piece of fabric). Finally, cut and fit the back chair back panel, which should be as long as the skirt. Ensure all seam allowances are trimmed to 2.5cm/1in before unpinning the calico. Use the pattern pieces to cut the main fabric.

pleated chair back panel

Fastened with buttons and tabs, this is a distinctive, modern finish for the back of a chair cover. Quick and easy to remove for washing, it is an ideal choice for a family home. Use toning buttons or cover them in the same fabric as the chair.

you will need

- **calico pattern**
- **washable fabric**
- **small, sharp scissors**
- **3 buttons or self-cover button kit**
- **sewing kit**

tips for pleated chair back panel

- Make a calico pattern first to ensure you understand the instructions before cutting into your fabric.
- For a different effect, attach a tie to each side of the pleat and tie into a bow.

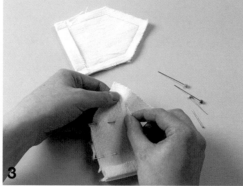

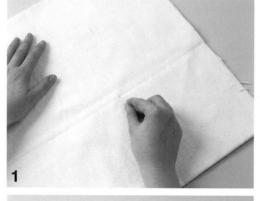

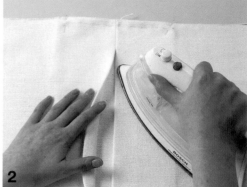

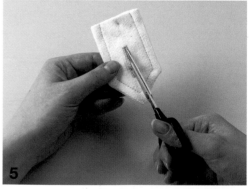

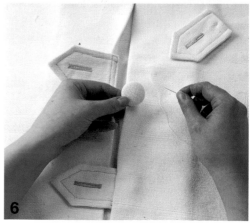

1 To make the pleat in the back panel, cut one piece of fabric 36cm/14in wider than the chair back and the same length, adding seam allowances all round. With right sides together, fold the back panel in half widthways and press. Measure 18cm/7in from the fold and tack (baste) along the 18cm/7in line. Stitch 2.5cm/1in down from the top edge, reinforcing the stitches at each end.

2 Open the pleat out so that the pressed foldline is centred behind the tacked seam. Press the pleat, then tack it in place across the top edge. Press again. Try the panel on the back of the chair and adjust to fit. Remove the tacking threads from the front of the pleat and press again.

3 Cut six tabs, each 8 x 12cm/3 x 4¾in. Cut a right-angled point at one end. Press under 1cm/½in along the short straight end of each tab. With right sides together, pin three sets of two tabs. Stitch a 1cm/½in seam around the raw edges. Trim the tab seams and cut across the corners.

4 Turn the tabs through and ease out the points. Top-stitch 5mm/¼in from the stitched edge, leaving the pressed-under edge free of stitching.

5 Mark the length of the buttonhole on each tab and stitch by machine. Cut along the centre of each buttonhole with a small pair of sharp scissors.

6 Pin the three tabs on the inside edge of the pleat, alternating them from side to side. Stitch the end of each tab securely to the inside edge only. Cover three buttons with fabric. Mark the position of each on the opposite edge to correspond with the buttonholes and stitch in place.

adding corner pleats

Corner pleats add fullness to the skirt of a slip cover and allow the person sitting in the chair to tuck their legs underneath without straining the seams. The calico pattern is extended to include the extra fabric required for the pleats before cutting the main fabric. If the fabric needs to be joined, make the seam down one of the inside edges of the pleat. Insert a zipper down one back corner seam.

above *Piping defines the chair seat, providing a clearer "fit".*

you will need

- calico pattern
- fabric
- sewing kit
- piping cord (optional)

tip for adding corner pleats
Cut the back skirt and back chair back as one continuous length for a professional finish.

1 To make the skirt pattern, measure from one back leg around the front of the chair to the other back leg. Add 60cm/24in to the total length for the pleats, and use to cut out the main fabric. Fold into three equal lengths, then press. Measure 15cm/6in in from each pressed fold and tack (baste) along the 15cm/6in line, through the two layers nearest the fold. Stitch 5cm/2in from the top edge, along the tacking line.

2 Open out the pleat so that the pressed line lies behind the stitch line. Tack along the top edge then stitch above the seamline to hold the fabric pleat. Press the pleat folds.

3 Add piping to the edge of the seat panel, if required. Pin the seat panel to the skirt, matching the centre line of each pleat to the front corners. Stitch the seam carefully, folding the skirt to the opposite side when you get to the centre seam of the pleat.

4 Attach the front of the chair back to the back edge of the seat and stitch the darts to shape the top corners or attach a gusset if required. Finally attach the back of the chair back, sandwiching piping between the two layers.

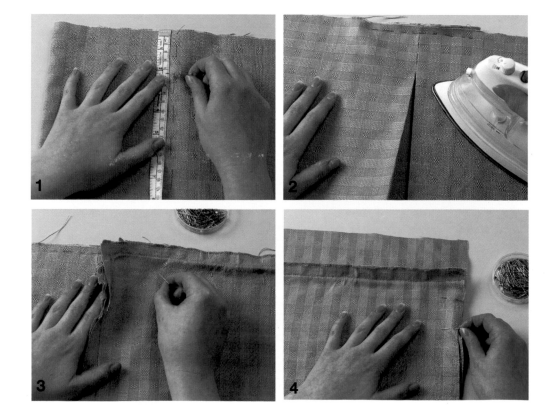

simple chair cover

This simple slipcover has darts at the top of the chair back instead of a gusset. Pin-fit calico to make a pattern, creating a seam between the seat and back. This seam continues round the edge of the chair, and is used to attach the front chair back to the back edge of the skirt. Fit a concealed zipper down one of the back seams. To fit a cover over a chair back that is wider at the top than the bottom, fit a zipper the full length of one of the back seams.

above *Darts make neat seams.*

you will need

- **calico pattern**
- **fabric**
- **invisible zipper**
- **sewing kit**

tip for simple chair cover

The skirt of this chair design is made in three pieces which have been stitched together. The back of the chair back extends down to complete the back of the skirt.

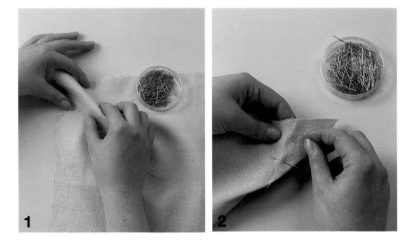

1 Cut out the fabric pieces, using the calico pattern. On the wrong side, fold and pin darts at the top corner of the front chair back. Tack (baste) in place, then check the fit on the chair.

2 Adjust the fit to ensure the fabric fits snugly over the thickness of the top of the chair. Stitch the darts in place and remove any pins or tacking stitches.

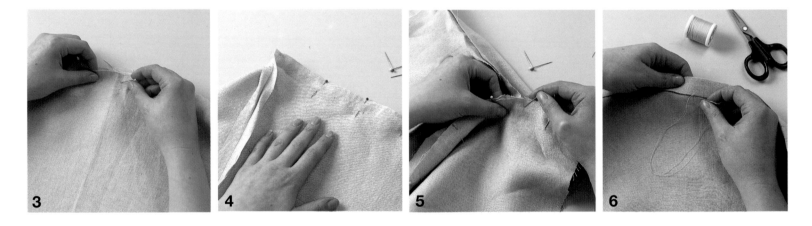

3 Pin the skirt panels together down the front seams. Stitch the seams and press open.

4 Pin the skirt around the two sides and along the front edge of the seat panel, making sure the front skirt seams are exactly on the corners. The skirt fabric will overhang the back edge of the seat panel at this stage. Stitch the seam, leaving the seam allowance free at the back edge.

5 Pin the front chair back panel to the seat panel, then on to the back edge of the skirt. This join needs to be pinned and stitched accurately, so that the three seams meet at a single point. Attach the back of the chair cover, inserting a zipper down one of the seams.

6 Fit the cover on the chair and mark the hem length. Turn up a double 2cm/¾in hem and slip-stitch.

adding a scallop edge and gusset

A gusset is the neatest way to fit a slipcover if the top edge of the chair back is shaped or curved. It is cut on the straight grain of the fabric and should be exactly the same thickness as the chair back plus seam allowances. Join the gusset at the corners of the chair back or in the centre of a curved edge, so that any pattern or nap doesn't end up upside down. Drawing round a small plate or saucer is a simple way to create an evenly scalloped edge. Plan the design so that it finishes neatly at the corners of the chair.

you will need

- **calico pattern**
- **main fabric**
- **lining fabric**
- **small plate**
- **pencil**
- **blunt tool**
- **sewing kit**

tip for adding a scallop edge and gusset

Continue the back of the chair back down to the same length as the chair skirt and cut matching scallops along the bottom edge.

1 Using the calico pattern, cut the gusset pattern pieces out of fabric so that the joins are in the least conspicuous position, and so that each gusset pattern piece matches the direction of the grain or pattern of the piece it will be joined to.

2 If the gusset panels are separate for the top and chair sides, stitch them together, beginning and finishing stitching a seam allowance' width from the raw edge of the fabric. Press the seams open.

3 Pin the gusset to the front of the chair back, matching the seams to the corners. Stitch up to the corner seam then, keeping the needle in the fabric, rotate the fabric until the next seam is lined up.

4 Attach the gusset panel to the chair back panel in the same way. Add the seat panel to the bottom of the front chair back.

5 Mark the length and width of each panel of the slipcover skirt, including the chair back, on a piece of lining. Divide the panel by the number of scallops and find a small plate to fit. Mark the shape of the scallops along the bottom edge.

6 With right sides together, stitch the skirt fabric to the lining along the pencil line. Add a lining to the skirt section of the chair back in the same way. Leave the sides and top edge open.

7 Trim the curved seam to 5mm/¼in. Notch the curved edge every 1–2cm/½–¾in. Snip into the point between each scallop.

8 Turn the skirt through and ease out the scallops with a blunt tool. Press the scalloped edge. Tack (baste), pin and stitch the skirt panels right sides together. Stitch the top edge of the skirt to the seat of the slipcover and the side edges to the chair back. Zigzag-stitch any raw edges.

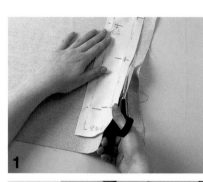

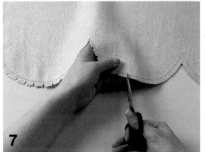
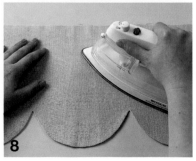

covering chairs and sofas

above *Loose covers for chairs are a practical option in a sitting room that receives a lot of hard wear and tear.*

Every piece of furniture is unique and each has its own fitting and sewing requirements, but the basic construction process is essentially the same for all. Measuring the furniture helps to plan the number and shape of the pattern pieces as well as estimating the amount of fabric you will require.

planning the cover

Decide where the seams will be on the slipcover. If it is to be similar to the upholstered version, the existing seam lines will probably suffice. For an alternative style, decide where the new seam lines will go and mark them on the chair with tailor's chalk. To enable the fabric to fit around the arms and lie neatly across the back, darts, tucks or a boxing strip need to be inserted. Which you choose will depend on the style of cover required but generally thicknesses over 8cm/3in need a boxing strip. Boxing strips give a formal,

geometric shape to furniture and the shape can be emphasized by inserting piping along the seams. Mark the seam lines for boxing strips on the furniture as a guide for measuring and pin-fitting.

measuring

Use the diagram to name all the different panels. Record the width and length of each piece and the number required. Select the widest and deepest points between the seam lines. It isn't necessary to measure every detail on a pattern, the pin-fitting will create the shape from the basic rectangle. For valances, measure the depth from the valance line and the circumference of the chair. Seam, hem and tuck-in allowances must be added to each piece and fullness for valances calculated. If the slipcover is a simple shape you can add these measurements to the pattern pieces but in general it is safer to add 10–20cm/4–8in to each side, ensuring that you have enough to adjust the shape and fit during pin-fitting.

calculating the yardage

Working with the oversize rectangles to be used for pin-fitting, draw a plan on graph paper. Use one square for 10cm/4in of fabric, and draw and cut out each piece required. On a second piece of graph paper use the same scale to draw two parallel lines to indicate the width of the fabric. If there is a prominent pattern or stripe, mark it on the graph paper to help arrange the pattern pieces. Label the pieces and arrange between the lines, in the most economical way possible, keeping the top of each piece facing in the same direction. Allow extra fabric for covering piping, buttons or other accessories. Count the squares and calculate the yardage from the scale used.

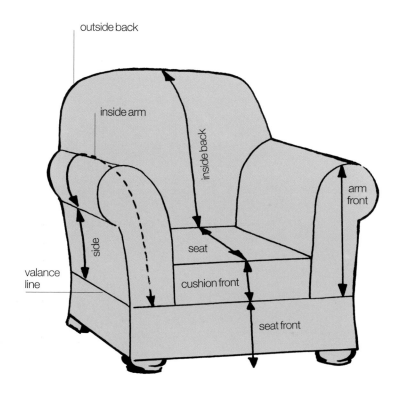

left *Label each pattern piece as you cut it and double check every measurement before cutting your fabric.*

making a pattern for a loose armchair cover

Creating a pattern by pin-fitting enables even the most inexperienced person to make a slipcover. Experienced soft-furnishers may be confident enough to work directly with the main fabric, but it is always safer to use a cheap, firm fabric such as calico to make a pattern first. You can then use the calico pattern to centre any design in the fabric on the main parts of the armchair. If you will be making a new cover that is identical to the style you are replacing, use the old cover as a pattern for the new fabric. Each armchair is different, so study the shape before deciding where the seams will lie – the seams of the slipcover do not have to match the seams of the upholstered cover. Try to keep the pieces as square as possible and to join panels on the straight grain of the fabric. Working in calico, you can alter the pattern pieces if you are not happy with the way the seams come together.

measuring up

Measure the armchair so that you can cut rough, oversize pieces of fabric for pin-fitting. Take as many measurements as you think necessary, removing the cushion to get the tape measure down on to the base of the seat. Draw a rough diagram of the chair, and record each measurement on it as you work.

you will need

• **tape measure**
• **paper and pencil**

1 For the inside back, measure horizontally across the inside back of the chair from edge to edge at the widest point, keeping the tape level.

2 Remove the cushion and mark with chalk where a valance will begin. Measure the seat front from the front edge of the chair to the chalk mark, then the width.

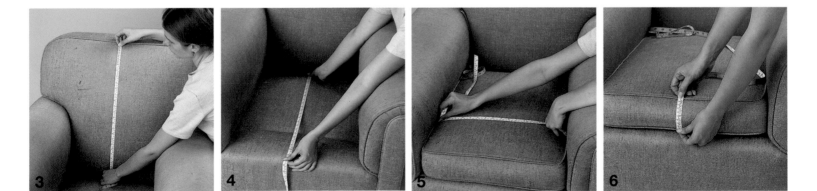

3 Measure down the centre back of the chair, from the top seam to the seat. Then measure the depth and length of the gusset sides and top.

4 Measure the length of the chair seat. Measure the outside chair back length to the chalked valance mark. Measure from the seat over the arm and down to the valance height on the side of the outside of the chair.

5 Replace the cushion pad, then measure the width and length between the arms across the seat. This measurement is used when cutting the seat panel of the slipcover and the seat cushion.

6 Measure the depth and length of the cushion pad. Finally, measure the length of the arm fronts.

pin-fitting a loose cover

Cut large rectangular pieces of calico, at least 10cm/4in larger all round than your measurements. The seam allowance around the seat is cut extra large and tucked in rather than stitched.

you will need
- **calico**
- **sewing kit**

tip for pin-fitting a loose cover

If it is necessary to join the calico, for example, to fit the width of a sofa, keep the seams centred or equally spaced at each side of the centre line.

1 Begin on the inside back. Place the first piece of calico over the chair so that it overhangs each seam. Pin it down the centre of the chair, keeping the straight grain vertical and pulling the fabric taut as you work.

2 Smooth the calico outwards and pin along the top edge. Work down the sides, tucking the fabric around the curve of the arms. Stand back and adjust any obvious discrepancies.

3 Carefully trim around the curve of the arm, leaving a generous seam allowance at this stage.

4 Place the next piece of calico over the arm of the chair so that it extends beyond the seat and to the bottom of the chair on the outside. Pin the fabric along the seam at the back of the arm. If you need to snip into the calico so that it lies flat, avoid cutting beyond the seam allowance.

5 Pin the gusset pieces together, and pin to the seam allowance of the arm and inside front panels. Pin the outside back panel on to the chair. Ease any fullness evenly across the back or around the corners of the chair.

6 Press a large sheet of paper over the front of the arm to get an imprint and cut a more accurate pattern from calico, with generous seam allowances. Pin-fit the arm front. Finally cut a panel of calico to fit inside the seat and down over the seat front.

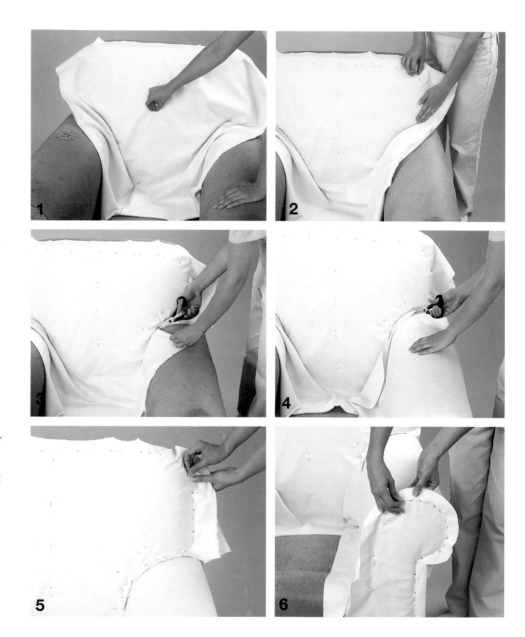

checking the pattern pieces

When the pin-fitting is complete, stand back and check that the cover looks balanced, and that the seams are straight. Check the width of the panels so that the cover matches from side to side, and adjust as necessary. Once you are satisfied, trim all the seams accurately to 2.5cm/1in, leaving a more generous 15cm/6in tuck-in allowance around the seat. Mark the pattern pieces on the right side with their name and position, for example, "left arm front" and "outside chair back". Unpin the pattern pieces and double-check that the "pairs" match in size. This is the last chance to make any major adjustments before cutting the main fabric.

making a loose armchair cover

The cover is made in the same order as the calico pattern was pin-fitted. Add a generous 15cm/6in tuck-in allowance around the edge of the seat if there wasn't sufficient to cut from the calico. Before stitching, it is a good idea to tack (baste) the main fabric pattern pieces together, and to fit them on to the chair the right way out so that you can check that the design (if any) matches and that no mistakes have been made. Mark the valance line at this point.

you will need
- **calico pattern**
- **fabric**
- **piping cord**
- **dressweight zipper**
- **sewing kit**

tip for making a loose armchair cover
Covering an armchair is a major undertaking but well within the scope of the competent sewer. If this is your first slipcover project, use a plain, self-coloured fabric to avoid potential problems with matching a pattern.

cutting out the pieces
To be on the safe side, cut the main fabric with the pattern pieces all facing the same way. This avoids potential problems with a pattern, or the pile of a nap fabric such as velvet, ending upside down.

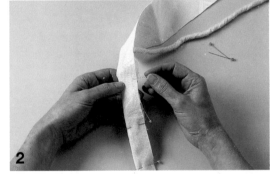

1 Pin all the calico pattern pieces on to the fabric, centring any design on the inside chair back and seat cushion. Use the pattern as a guide to match the design on the seat and arm fronts.

2 If any seams are to be piped, join strips to make a continuous length of fabric, wide enough to fit over the piping cord plus 2.5cm/1in seam allowance. Piping for slipcovers is usually cut on the bias, but it is better to cut it on the straight grain if the fabric is checked or has a distinct design.

3 Stitch the strips of fabric over the piping cord, using a zipper foot attachment. Pin the piping around the edge of each piece to be piped, with raw edges aligned, and stitch in place.

4 Stitch the fabric pieces together in the same way that the pattern was assembled. Stitch the inside back to the gusset panel, then add the outside back. Add the arms, leaving the left-hand seam between the back of the arm and the outside back open for a zipper. Stitch the tuck-in seams before attaching the seat front.

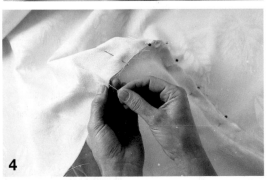

adding a gathered valance

This is the simplest way to finish the bottom of an armchair or sofa, giving a soft, casual appearance.

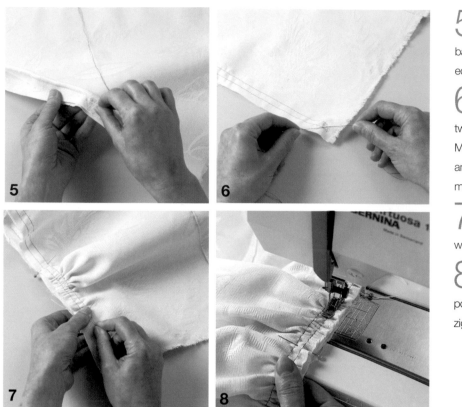

5 Trim the lower edge of the slipcover, leaving 2.5cm/1in seam allowance below the valance line mark. Mark the edges of the back opening for the zipper. Pin and tack (baste) piping along this edge, between the marks, around the bottom of the slipcover.

6 Measure the depth of valance required and add 5cm/2in seam and hem allowance. Cut and join strips of fabric to make a strip twice as long as the bottom edge. Turn up and stitch a 2cm/¾in hem. Measure and mark the valance into separate metres (yards) with pins and stitch two rows of gathering stitches between the metre (yard) marks. Tie the gathering thread off at one end of each section.

7 Measure every 50cm/20in around the bottom of the slipcover. Pin the valance to the slipcover, matching the metre (yard) marks with the 50cm/20in marks. Pull up the gathering threads.

8 Adjust the gathers evenly. Stitch the valance in place, using a zipper foot attachment so that you can stitch as close as possible to the piping cord. Remove the gathering threads and zigzag-stitch the raw edge.

adding a zipper

A zipper on the back of an armchair or sofa should be as inconspicuous as possible. Fit the zipper using the concealed method, down the left back seam. On a sofa, where the back panel has been joined, fit the zipper down the left seam on the back, using the semi-concealed method (see basic techniques).

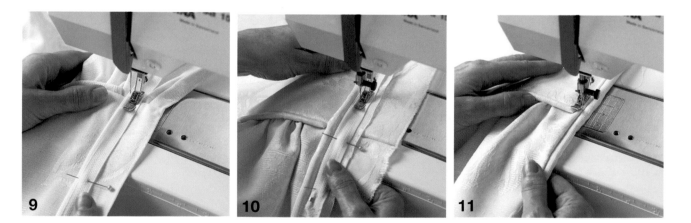

9 Fit the zipper into the gap left open down the back left-hand seam. Open the zipper and pin, face down, along the seamline on the back panel. Stitch, using a zipper foot.

10 Pin and stitch piping down the seamline on the outside arm section of the gap. Stitch the other half of the zipper in place over the piping.

11 Fold the zipper and seam allowance to the wrong side. Top-stitch close to the piping to hold the zipper in position. Fold and stitch the other side of the zipper in the same way.

right *A deep frilled valance adds a feminine and luxurious touch to a classic armchair cover.*

making a box-pleated valance

Box pleating is a more formal finish than a gathered valance. The box pleats can be full, so that the folds of the pleats meet at the front and the back, or they can be half-pleats with a gap in-between. Full pleats are more formal and use three times the finished length. Half-pleats need approximately twice the finished length.

To check the length and spacing required, cut a strip of calico and fold it to form whichever pleats you have chosen. Press the pleats and pin. Pin around the armchair and adjust to fit.

you will need
- **main fabric**
- **calico strip**
- **piping cord**
- **sewing kit**

tip for making a box-pleated valance
The spacing of the pleats can be adjusted slightly so that the edge of the pleat finishes at each corner.

1 Cut the valance fabric the required length and depth, adding 5cm/2in seam and hem allowance. Turn under 1cm/½in along the lower edge and then fold up another 1.5cm/⅝in. Stitch the double hem in place.

2 Open the calico strip to it's full length and use it as a pattern for spacing the pleats. Insert pins along both edges of the main fabric to mark the foldlines of the pleats. Arrange the pleats so that the edge of one pleat will finish at each end of the front of the armchair or sofa.

3 Fold the valance at each of the pins to make the box pleats. Press the edges of each batch of pleats with a steam iron and leave to cool before moving them. Tack (baste) the bottom of the pleats temporarily.

4 Cover a length of piping with fabric and pin it along the top edge of the valance. Fold the end of the piping over at the left-hand seamline where the zipper is to be inserted. Pin the valance along the valance line on the slipcover and stitch securely in place. Zigzag-stitch any raw edge and press upwards.

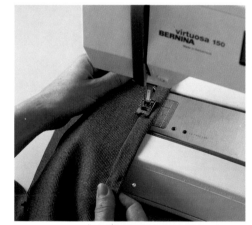

semi-fitted cover for a tub chair

Modern tub chairs look much better with a semi-fitted cover that is halfway between a loose cover and an upholstered cover. The pieces for the cover are assembled in the same way as for a traditional armchair, but the cover is held in place underneath the chair with a cord that runs through a casing.

Pin-fit calico to create a pattern, then cut out the fabric panels. Allow 10–12.5cm/4–5in along the bottom edge for the casing. Fitting is easier on a tub chair if two seams are added on the inside and outside chair back panels. Insert a zipper behind the piping on the back left-hand seam.

you will need

- **fabric**
- **piping cord**
- **thin cord**
- **upholstery zipper**
- **sewing kit**

tip for semi-fitted cover for a tub chair
Use a loose weave or stretch fabric for this style of chair so that the fabric can stretch slightly to fit the curved back edge.

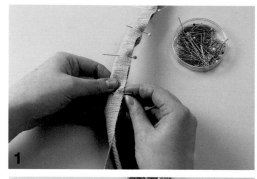

1 Using the chair fabric, cut sufficient continuous bias binding to fit along all the seams of the chair, except those around the seat. Fold the binding over the piping cord and pin. Stitch close to the edge of the cord, using a zipper foot.

2 Pin the piping on the right side of all the relevant cover pieces. Snip into the piping seam allowance if necessary to ease the piping around any tight curves, such as at the top of the arm fronts.

3 Stitch the cover pieces together. The seat seam is stitched without piping, instead of being tucked in like a traditional armchair. Fit the cover and mark the position of the legs with pins. Lift the cover off and draw a smooth curve with tailor's chalk. Cut along the chalk line.

4 Zigzag-stitch or overcast the raw edge of the curve and turn to the reverse side. Top-stitch the curve to secure. Turn up and stitch a 1.5cm/⅝in hem along the bottom edge to make a casing. Thread the cord through the casing, leaving loops in the gaps to fit over the legs of the chair.

5 Insert a zipper behind a piped edge in the left-hand back seam. Leave the other side plain. Fit the cover over the chair and pull the cord tight. Tie the cord in a double bow to secure and tuck up inside the cover.

covering a square or rectangular footstool

The method of covering a footstool depends very much on the design and the way the stool is constructed. This footstool is covered with a simple drawstring covering for the cushion and a semi-fitted base. Its success relies on accurate cutting and perfect fitting.

you will need

- **calico pattern**
- **heavyweight furnishing fabric**
- **thin cord**
- **strong thread or Velcro**
- **sewing kit**

tip for covering a square or rectangular footstool

Pre-shrink fabric before making a close-fitting cover like this, as you may find it will not fit after cleaning.

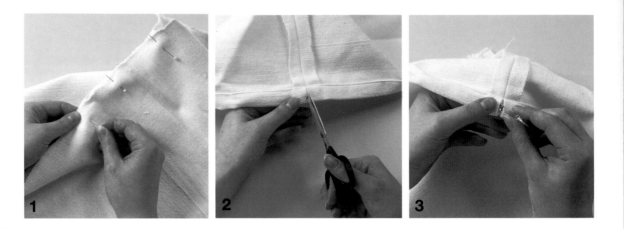

1 Cut the fabric for the cushion top, adding 1.5cm/⅝in seam allowances all around. Measure the cushion sides and cut four strips the same length plus seam allowances plus 5cm/2in deeper. Stitch the side seams into one piece, starting and finishing a seam allowance' width from each raw edge. Pin the sides to the top and stitch in place.

2 Turn up a 2cm/¾in double hem around the bottom edge and stitch in place. Snip into the casing at one of the corner seams.

3 Cut a length of cord to fit around the footstool and thread it through the gap in the hem. Fit the cover over the cushion. Pull up the cord tightly and tie on the underside.

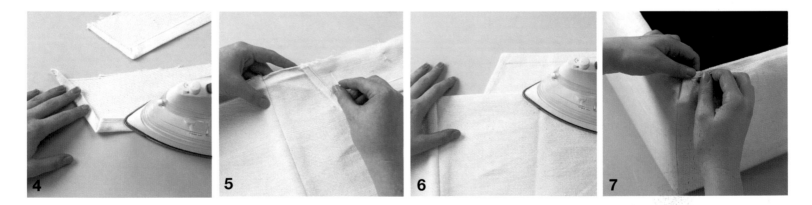

4 Cut four panels of fabric to fit each side of the base, adding 1.5cm/⅝in seam allowance to the sides and bottom edge and 5cm/2in along the top. With right sides together, stitch the short sides and press the seams open. Cut four strips, each 10cm/4in wide, to fit as flaps between the legs of the footstool. Trim the ends of each strip at an angle and press under 1cm/⅜in along the sides and bottom edge. Turn up another 1.5cm/⅝in on the bottom edge to form a casing to thread a cord through and stitch. Top-stitch the flaps.

5 Pin the flaps along the bottom edge, leaving a gap to each side of the side seams for the legs of the footstool. Stitch each in place.

6 Neaten the seam allowances with zigzag stitch and press the flaps outwards. At the top raw edge of the base cover, turn under 1.5cm/⅝in, press and top-stitch. Fit the cover on to the base. Thread a thin cord through the casing of the flaps and pull tightly under the base to secure a snug fit.

7 Pin the top edge of the base cover, mitring the corners neatly. Oversew the corner seams by hand, using a strong thread. Alternatively, secure the top edge with Velcro. To do this stitch strips of loop Velcro along the top edge of the footstool cover. Hand stitch or staple hook Velcro around the top outside edge of the footstool.

loose cover with pockets for a round footstool

A footstool without a cushion is firm enough to double as an occasional table. It can easily be transformed into a mini-workstation with ample storage space for scissors, tape measure and other sewing equipment.

you will need
- calico pattern
- mediumweight furnishing fabric
- lining if necessary
- large buttons
- small, sharp scissors
- thin cord
- sewing kit

tip for loose cover with pockets for a round footstool
A wicker footstool can be covered with wadding (batting) to soften the surface before covering with fabric. Alternatively, cut a circle of firm crumble foam to make a more comfortable seat.

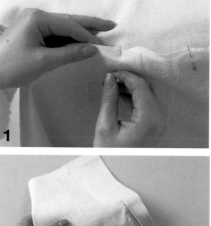

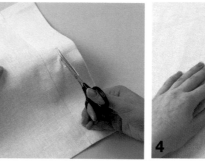

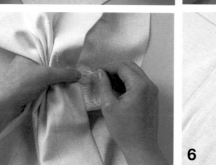

1 Measure the footstool. Cut a circle of fabric for the top and a strip of fabric to fit around the footstool, adding 2.5cm/1in seam allowance on all edges. Pin-fit the cover to check the size.

2 Decide on the finished size of the pockets, adding 1.5cm/⅝in seam allowance to the sides and bottom and 12cm/4¾in for the hem. Turn under a small seam allowance along the top edge. Press and stitch. With right sides together turn the folded edge down by 10cm/4in. Press, stitch each side and turn through.

3 Top-stitch the hem, then turn in the seam allowance and press. Mark the position of the buttonhole on the top edge of each pocket and stitch. Cut along the centre of each buttonhole with a pair of sharp scissors.

4 Lay the side fabric flat and space the pockets evenly along the length. Position so that the bottom edge of the pocket lies along the lower edge of the footstool. Pin and stitch the pockets in place.

5 Sew a button behind each buttonhole. Stitch the side seam and press open. Pin the circle of fabric for the footstool top in place with right sides together and stitch. Zigzag-stitch the raw edges to neaten them.

6 Turn up a 5mm/¼in hem at the bottom edge. Press, then turn up another 2cm/¾in hem. Stitch in place. At the seam unpick a few stitches to make a gap to thread a length of thin cord through. Fit the cover and pull the cord tight underneath.

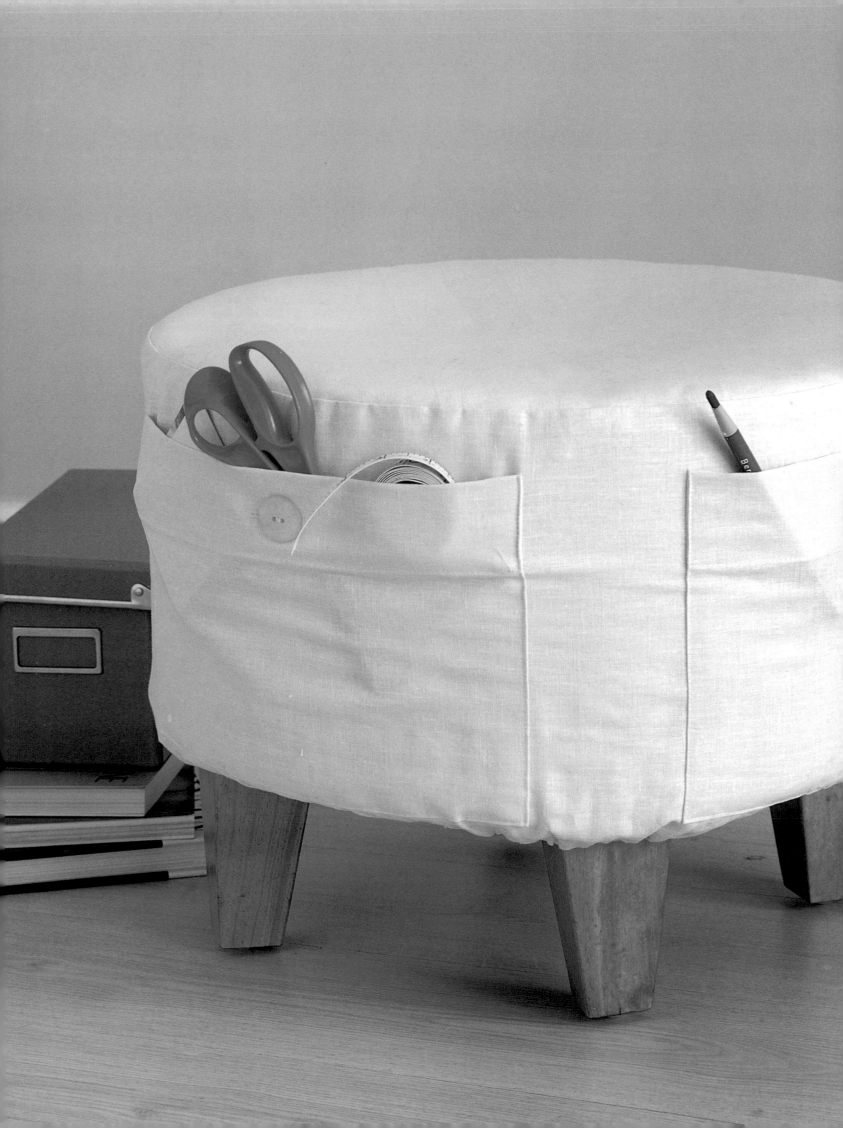

covering a deckchair

Deckchair canvas often begins to perish after a few years, long before the frame is showing signs of wear. This method of attaching a new cover using eyelets to fasten the turning is quick and easy. The eyelets can be threaded with a colourful cord.

you will need
- **deckchair canvas**
- **pencil and ruler**
- **eyelet tool**
- **bodkin (optional)**
- **5mm/¼in eyelets**
- **hammer**
- **thick, coloured cord**
- **sewing kit**

tip for covering a deckchair

Canvas can be bought in a standard width for deckchairs. If you want to use an alternative fabric, fold and stitch a narrow double hem down each side before fitting.

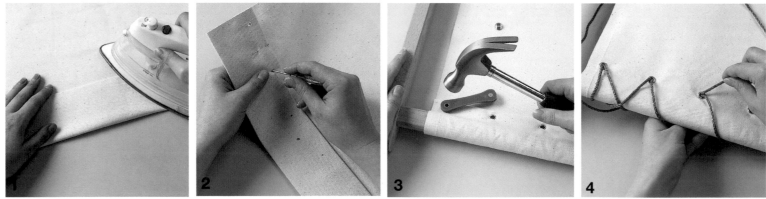

1 Measure the length between the outside edge of the bars when the deckchair is flat and add 32cm/12¾in hem allowance to the length. Turn under a double 8cm/3in hem at each short end of the fabric and press.

2 Mark the position of the eyelets approximately 6cm/2⅛in apart. Cut holes for the eyelets, using an eyelet tool or the point of a pair of sharp scissors. If the canvas is too thick, use a bodkin to make a hole.

3 Place the chair face down and fold the hem over the bar. Insert the tube section of the eyelet from the right side and fit the ring on top. Hammer into position through all the layers, following the manufacturer's instructions.

4 Thread the cord through the eyelets, either working a row of back stitch or crossing the cord over the top of the bar to make a decorative pattern. Knot the ends at one edge on the back of the chair.

covering a director's chair

As with deckchairs, the covers on wooden chairs often wear out long before the chair itself needs replacing. If you use the old cover as a pattern, remember to make some allowance if the fabric has stretched out of shape. If you are not using striped fabric for the new cover, draw parallel lines on the fabric with a ruler as a guide for stitching the quilting lines.

you will need

- **calico pattern**
- **mediumweight furnishing fabric**
- **wadding (batting)**
- **sewing kit**

tip for covering a director's chair
Use the old cover as a guide for sewing and fitting the new seat cover.

1 Make a calico pattern, then measure the depth needed for the chair back and the length from one strut to the other, around the strut and back again. Cut the chair back from fabric, adding 1.5cm/⅝in seam allowance all round. Fold the fabric in half, right sides together, and stitch the short ends together. Press the seam open, then rotate the seam so that it is 6cm/2½in from the right-hand side. Press under 1.5cm/⅝in along the long edges.

2 Top-stitch through all layers 5cm/2in from both side edges to make channels for the chair back struts. Stitch another line 5mm/¼in from the first.

3 Cut a piece of wadding (batting) to fit inside the back panel. Tuck the wadding under the seam allowances on the front of the panel and pin. Tack (baste) the layers together with lines radiating out from the centre.

4 Using a quilting or clear-view foot on the sewing machine, stitch down the stripes to quilt the panel and to close the top and bottom seams. Stitch all the lines in the same direction. Alternatively mark parallel lines 3cm/1¼in apart. Make the seat panel in the same way. Remove the tacking stitches.

covering a plastic garden chair

Plastic chairs make cheap and hard-wearing seating but they do not always look attractive, especially if used as additional seating beside a wooden or wrought iron table. Transform them with simple fitted covers and co-ordinated seat pads, which can easily be removed and taken indoors at night. The size of the cover pieces is worked out using the pin-fitting method for dining chairs. Because you cannot insert pins into the plastic, use tape to hold the first panels in position.

you will need

- **light- or mediumweight cotton fabric**
- **adhesive tape**
- **self-cover button kit**
- **sewing kit**
- **paper and pencil to make a pattern**
- **calico and stuffing or thick foam**

tip for covering a plastic garden chair
Use a contrast piping around the seat cushion to give a professional finish.

1 Cut the fabric panels for the cover oversize and fit them to the chair, using tape to hold them in position. Cut the outside back and sides in one piece of fabric. Also cut the seat and front panels in one piece so that there is no seam at the front edge.

2 Pin-fit the inside back seams, making sure that any design is balanced on both sides. When you are satisfied with the fit, trim the seam allowance to exactly 2.5cm/1in along all seams. Stitch the sections together with a 2.5cm/1in seam allowance, leaving a gap down both front seams from the seat to the floor.

3 Cut a 4 x 30cm/1½ x 12in strip of fabric for the button tabs. With wrong sides together, press the long edges of the strip into the centre then fold it in half again.

4 Stitch the strip close to the folded edge. Cut it to make two lengths, each 14cm/5½in. Fold each tab in half and press into shape.

5 Fold over and press a 1cm/½in hem along each edge of the gaps in the skirt front seams. Mark the position of the tabs on the front edges of the side piece, 20cm/8in from the seat edge. Tuck the ends of each tab under the hem and pin. Check that the buttons fit the tabs. Stitch the hem.

6 Fold each tab out over the edge. Top-stitch a decorative triangle to secure and strengthen it. Turn up and pin the bottom hem of the cover, then stitch. Sew buttons on the opposite side of each skirt gap to match the position of the tabs.

7 Draw a paper pattern for the seat cushion. Make a box cushion pad or have a piece of thick foam cut to size. Make a cover for the cushion, following the instructions for the box-style shaped cushion.

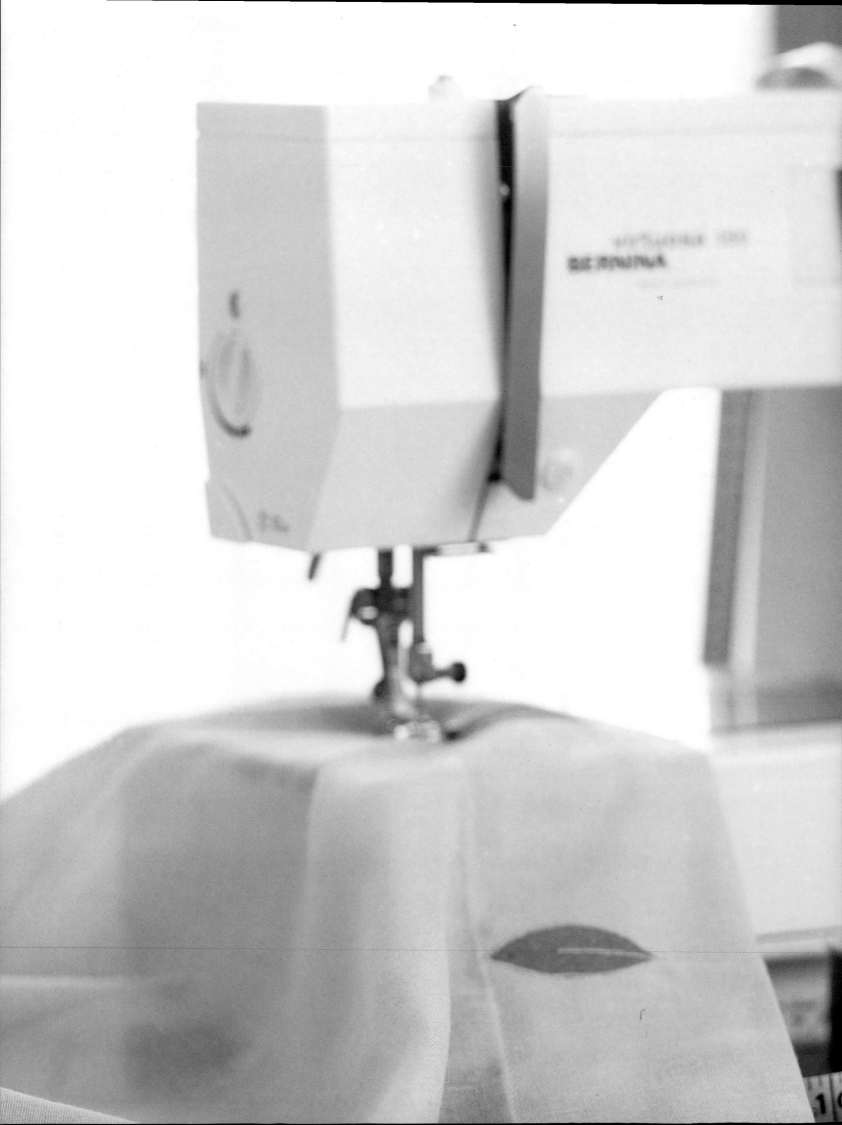

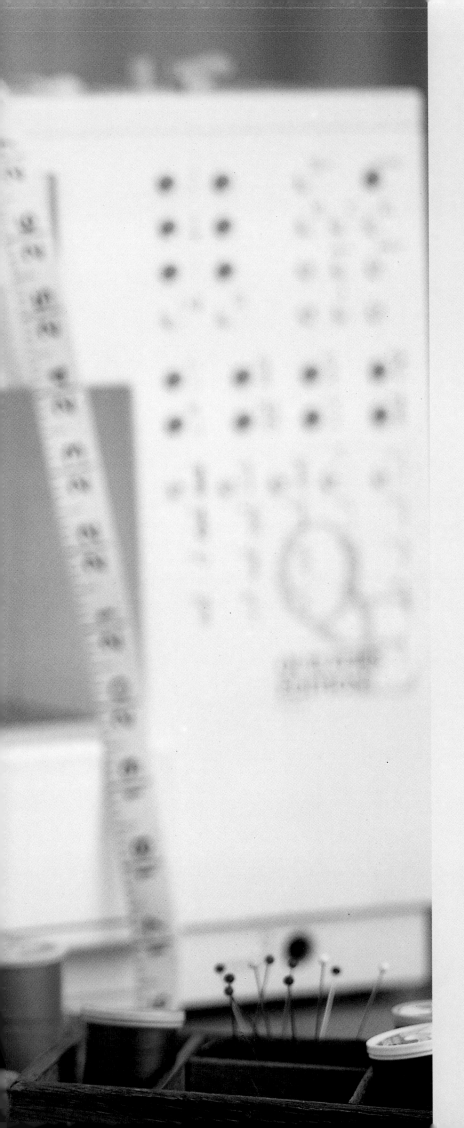

basic techniques

Technique makes the difference between something that looks average and something that looks immaculately tailored, with a crisp, professional finish. Take time to learn the basic techniques in the following pages – they will help you achieve perfect results that you can be proud of.

the sewing kit

You will probably have much of this equipment already in your sewing box. Check that the scissors you use for cutting fabric are perfectly sharp and do not use them for any other purpose.

1 Bodkin
Used to thread elastic, cord or ribbon through casings.

2 Dressmaker's carbon and tracing wheel
Used together to transfer markings to the wrong side of the fabric. Select carbon paper that is close in colour to the fabric colour but still visible. Always use white carbon paper on white fabric (it shows as a dull line).

3 Fabric markers
A pencil is suitable for marking most hard-surfaced fabrics and can be brushed off with a stiff brush. A vanishing-ink pen will wash out in water or fade. Use a tracing pen to draw a design on waxed paper and then transfer it to the fabric by ironing over it.

4 Fusible bonding web
This glue mesh is used to stick two layers of fabric together. It is available in various widths. The narrow bands shown here are useful for heavyweight hems and facings, and the wider widths are used for appliqué.

5 Hand-sewing needles
"Sharps" (medium-length, all-purpose needles) are used for general hand sewing. For fine hand sewing, use the shorter, round-eyed "betweens". Hand-sewing needles are numbered from 1–10, with 10 being the finest.

6 Pincushion
Useful for holding pins and needles as you work.

7 Dressmaker's pins
Use normal household pins for most sewing, and lace pins for delicate fabrics. Glass-headed pins are easy to see.

8 Quilter's tape
Used to mark very accurate seam allowances. The tape is 5mm/¼in wide but can be placed further from the raw edge to stitch wider seams.

9 Rouleau turner
A metal tool used to turn through rouleau loops.

10 Safety pins
Use to hold thick layers of fabric together.

11 Scissors
You will need a large pair of drop-handle (bent-handle) scissors for cutting out fabric, a medium pair for trimming seams or cutting small pieces of fabric, and a small pair of sharp, pointed embroidery scissors for cutting threads and snipping into curves. Never cut paper with sewing scissors as it dulls the blade.

12 Seam ripper
A small cutting tool for undoing machine-stitching mistakes. Also useful for cutting buttonholes.

13 Tape measure
Buy a 150cm/60in tape with metal tips in a material such as fibreglass that will not stretch. A small metal ruler with an adjustable guide is useful when pinning hems, tucks and buttonholes.

14 Tailor's chalk
Used to mark fabric. Keep the edge sharp by shaving it with medium scissors. Test on the right side of the fabric to ensure it will brush off.

15 Thimble
Worn on the middle finger of your sewing hand to prevent accidental needle pricks when hand sewing.

16 Sewing threads
For best results, choose a thread that matches the fibre content of the fabric. Use a shade of thread that matches the fabric. If there is no match go one shade darker. Use strong thread for furnishing fabrics and for hand quilting. Tacking (basting) thread is cheaper and poorer-quality. Use strong buttonhole twist or linen thread for buttonholes.

17 Tissue paper
When machine stitching delicate fabrics, tack (baste) strips of tissue paper to each side of the seam and stitch as normal. Tear the tissue paper off afterwards.

the sewing machine

For soft furnishings, a sturdy flat-bed sewing machine is the most suitable kind but any ordinary domestic machine can be used.

Balance wheel
This controls the sewing machine. On manual machines, turn the wheel to lower the needle.

Bobbin winder
This allows you to fill the bobbin quickly and evenly.

Foot control or knee control
This starts, stops and controls the speed at which the machine stitches.

Needle clamp
This secures the shaft of the needle into the machine.

Needle plate
The needle plate surrounds the feed teeth and has a hole for the needle.

Presser foot
This holds the fabric flat on the needle plate so that a stitch can form.

Stitch length control
Use this to alter the length of straight stitches and the density of zigzag stitch.

Stitch width control
This controls the amount the needle moves sideways. Use a suitable presser foot so that the needle doesn't break as it swings from side to side.

Thread take-up lever
This feeds the correct amount of thread from the spool down through to the needle.

Tension regulating dial
The tension dial alters the tension on the top thread.

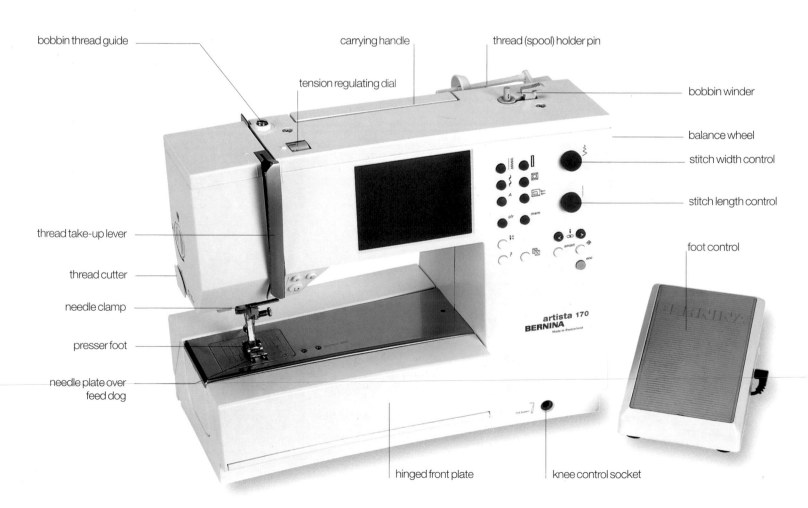

bobbin thread guide

carrying handle

thread (spool) holder pin

tension regulating dial

bobbin winder

balance wheel

stitch width control

stitch length control

thread take-up lever

thread cutter

needle clamp

presser foot

foot control

needle plate over feed dog

artista 170
BERNINA
Made in Switzerland

hinged front plate

knee control socket

Thread cutter

This is situated at the back of the sewing machine for cutting threads.

Thread (spool) holder pin

This holds the reel (spool) of thread when filling the bobbin and stitching.

MACHINE NEEDLES

Always select a machine needle to suit the fabric and the thread you are using; this will reduce the possibility of the needle breaking.

Universal needles

Universal sewing machine needles range in size from 70/9, used for fine fabrics, to 110/18, used for heavyweight fabrics. Size 80/12 is ideal for a mediumweight fabric. Keep a selection of needles to hand and change the needle when using a different weight of fabric. A fine needle will break if the fabric is too thick, and a large needle will damage a fine fabric.

Embroidery needles

These needles have larger eyes than normal to accommodate a wide range of decorative threads (floss). Keep a separate needle for each type of thread because the thread creates a groove on the needle that will cause other threads to break.

Top-stitch and jean-point needles

Special top-stitch needles have a very large eye to accommodate a thicker thread, although top stitching can also be worked using the same thread as the main fabric. Jean-point needles have a specially elongated sharp point to stitch through heavyweight fabrics.

Fitting the needle

Machine needles can only be fitted one way as they have a flat surface down one side (the shank) and a long groove down the other side (the shaft). When the needle is inserted, this groove should line up directly with the last thread guide. When the machine is in use, the thread runs down the groove and scores a unique channel into the metal. So when you change thread, you should change your needle, too.

| zipper foot | clear-view foot | general all-purpose foot | buttonhole foot |

MACHINE FEET

All sewing machines have interchangeable feet for different types of sewing. These are designed for particular functions such as stitching close to a zipper or piping cord. The most common ones are illustrated here, but you can buy other specialist (specialty) feet.

General-purpose foot The basic metal general-purpose foot is used for all general straight and zigzag stitching on ordinary fabrics.

Clear-view foot Similar to the general-purpose foot, this foot allows you to see where you are stitching. It can be cut away or made from clear plastic. Use for machine quilting or appliqué.

Zipper foot This allows you to stitch close to the zipper teeth, and to piping cord. On some, the needle can be adjusted to sew on either side. A special zipper foot is available for invisible zippers.

Buttonhole foot This foot has a metal strip to guide rows of satin stitch forwards and backwards, leaving a tiny gap between for cutting the buttonhole.

STITCH TENSION

A new sewing machine should have the tension correctly set, with the dial at the marked centre point. Try out any stitches you intend to use on a sample of the fabric.

To check the tension, bring all the pattern and zigzag dials back to zero and set the stitch length between 2 and 3 for normal stitching. Place a folded strip of fabric on the needle plate, lower the needle into the fabric and sew a row of straight stitches. These should look exactly the same on both sides.

Altering the tension

To tighten the tension, turn the dial towards the lower numbers; to loosen it, turn towards the higher numbers. This will automatically affect the tension of the thread coming through the bobbin case. If the top tension dial is far from the centre, the spring on the bobbin case is probably wrong.

Only alter the lower tension as a last resort. You should be able to dangle the bobbin case without the thread slipping through. Shake the thread and the bobbin case should drop a little. Turn the screw on the side of the bobbin case slightly to alter the tension. Test the stitching again on a sample of fabric and alter the top tension this time until the stitches are perfect.

maintenance and trouble-shooting

Like a car, a sewing machine will only run well if it is used frequently and looked after. Cleaning is essential when you change fabrics, especially from a dark to a light-coloured one. Remove the sewing machine needle. Use a stiff brush to clean out the fluff (lint) along the route the top thread takes through the machine. Unscrew the needle plate and brush out any fluff from around the feed teeth. Remove the bobbin case to check that no thread is trapped in the mechanism.

above *Immaculately-tailored seams will ensure your soft furnishing items last longer as well as look better.*

Oil the machine from time to time, following the instructions in your handbook. Only use a couple of drops of oil. Leave the machine overnight with a fabric pad beneath the presser foot, then wipe the needle before use. Some new machines are self-lubricating. Even if you take good care of your machine, problems can occur. Some of the more common problems are listed below.

The machine works too slowly
The machine may have two speeds and may be set on slow. More likely, it hasn't been used for a while and oil could be clogging the working parts. Run the machine without a needle for a minute to loosen all the joints. Check that the foot control is not obstructed. As a last resort, ask a dealer to check the tension belt.

No stitches form
Ensure that the bobbin is full and inserted correctly. Check that the needle is facing in the right direction and threaded from the grooved side.

The needle doesn't move
Check first of all that the balance wheel is tight and that the bobbin winder is switched off. If the needle still doesn't move, the problem may be caused by thread trapped in the sewing hook behind the bobbin case. Remove the bobbin case and take hold of the thread end. Rock the balance wheel backwards and forwards until the thread comes out.

left *A professional look to soft furnishings is a result of seams stitched with perfect tension and no puckers.*

The machine jams

Rock, but don't force, the balance wheel gently to loosen the threads and take the fabric out. Remove the needle, unscrew the needle plate and brush out any fluff (lint). Alternatively, check that the machine is correctly threaded and that the fabric is far enough under the presser foot when you begin stitching.

The needle bends or breaks

A needle will break if it hits the foot, bobbin case or needle plate. Check that you are using the correct foot. When using a zipper foot, a common mistake is forgetting to move the needle to the left or right for straight or zigzag-stitching. Check the bobbin case is inserted properly. Make sure the take-up lever is at its highest point before fitting.

A needle that has been bent will break if it hits the needle plate. To avoid bent needles, sew slowly over pins and thick seams. A needle will also bend if there is a knot in the thread, or if the fabric is pulled through the machine faster than the machine is sewing. Replace bent needles immediately.

The fabric does not feed through

This can happen when the feed teeth are lowered in the darning or machine embroidery position. Close zigzag or embroidery stitches will bunch up in the general-purpose foot, so change the foot to one that is cut away underneath to allow the stitches to feed through. Check also that the machine is correctly threaded.

The stitches are different lengths

Check whether the needle is blunt or unsuitable for the fabric and that it is inserted correctly. (Test this on a scrap of fabric before beginning the project.) Try stitching with the needle in the left or right position. On fine fabrics, put tissue paper under the presser foot.

The top thread keeps breaking

Manufacturers recommend that you change needles every time you change the type of thread. This is because each thread wears a unique groove in the needle as it is being stitched. Label your needle packet to indicate what type of thread to use with each needle. This is particularly important when doing machine embroidery. Check also that you are using the correct thread and type of needle for the fabric. A knot or slub in the thread or an over-tight top tension can also cause the thread to break.

above *A well maintained sewing machine is an indispensable tool for making soft furnishings.*

The bobbin thread breaks

Check that the bobbin case is inserted correctly, has not been over-filled, and that the thread has no knots in it. Also check the bobbin case mechanism for trapped fluff (lint). Occasionally, the spring on the bobbin case is too tight for the thread and the tension screw needs to be loosened – refer to your manual for instructions.

choosing fabrics

If one of your soft furnishing projects isn't successful, it could be your choice of fabric or the way you handled it that lets it down. With such a wonderful range of fabrics on the market, there is no need for "hand-made" to mean a cheaper alternative or second-best. Staff in most fabric shops will be pleased to pass on their knowledge about choosing the best fabric for a particular purpose.

PREPARING FABRIC

Once you have chosen the fabric, the temptation is to start cutting straight away. Curb your enthusiasm, however – a little time spent preparing the fabric before you begin will help prevent costly mistakes later.

Before beginning any soft furnishing project, the first thing to do is to straighten the fabric. When fabric is wrapped around a large bolt or roll, it can be pulled slightly out of shape and this may not become obvious until you have already started sewing. Problems such as the pattern not matching, cushion covers that aren't square, curtains not hanging straight, or a swag draping incorrectly can all be caused by the fabric being slightly off-grain.

To check whether the fabric is straight or off-grain, first straighten the ends, either by tearing the fabric or by pulling a thread (see below), then fold it in half lengthways with the selvages together to see if the two crossways ends meet squarely. Sometimes it isn't obvious that the fabric is not straight because the bolt was used as a guide for cutting in the store, which can make the end look straight. Always check it anyway – it will help to ensure perfect results.

left *Always choose fabrics that are suitable for the job in hand.*

STRAIGHTENING FABRIC ENDS

If the fabric has an obvious weave, or a woven pattern such as a check, it can easily be cut along the grain to ensure it is straight. In most cases, however, you will have to tear or cut along a thread to guarantee a straight line.

Tearing is the quickest way to straighten a fabric end but this is only suitable for plain-weave fabrics such as calico or poplin. Try a test piece first to ensure that tearing the fabric won't harm it, or cause it to tear lengthways. The safest way to straighten the end is by pulling a thread. This takes longer, but is worth it.

1 Look carefully at the weave of the fabric and snip into the selvage next to where the first thread goes straight across. Pull one of the crossways threads until the fabric gathers up.

2 Ease the gathers gently along the thread as far as possible, then cut carefully along this line. Continue this process until you have cut right across the fabric.

STRAIGHTENING THE GRAIN

Once the end of the fabric is straight, you will be able to check if the fabric is off-grain. There are two ways to do this. You can either lay the fabric flat on a square table or fold it in half lengthways with the selvages together. In both cases, the ends should be square. If the corners don't match, the fabric needs to be straightened before you can begin cutting and sewing. If it is only slightly off-grain it can be steam-pressed into shape, but misshapen fabric must be pulled back into shape. This can be quite hard work for a large piece of fabric, and you may need to enlist the help of a friend to pull from the opposite end. This step is essential and will affect the final drape of the fabric, so don't be tempted to miss this stage.

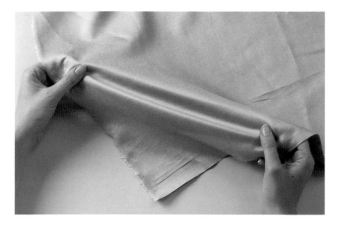

To pull the fabric back into shape, hold it firmly on each side of the narrow corners and pull your hands apart. Keep moving your hands down each side, pulling firmly until you reach the other corners. This is easier to do if two people work from opposite corners. Fold the fabric in half lengthways, right sides together. Pin the raw edges together. Place pins into the ironing board every 13cm/5in along the selvage. Press the fabric from the selvage into the fold until the weave is absolutely straight, but avoid pressing the fold. Leave the fabric to cool before removing the pins. For pressing large pieces of fabric cover a table with a blanket and sheet.

fabric terminology

It is important to understand the terms used when describing fabric. Some fabrics handle very differently if cut on the crossways grain rather than the lengthways grain, and designs can end up facing in the wrong direction. Most fabrics are cut with the right sides of the fabric together, and can be folded on the lengthways or crossways fold. Nap designs have a design or surface texture, which means that the fabric must be folded lengthways or not at all.

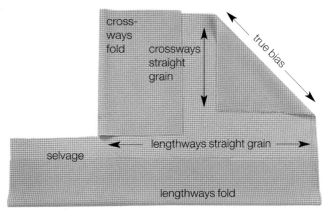

Bias

The bias is any diagonal line across woven fabric. Bias strips are used for binding or piping curved edges. Fabric cut on the bias has more stretch than fabric cut on the straight grain, and the most stretch is achieved on the true bias; this is when the selvage edge on one side is folded over to run parallel to the crossways grain.

Fold

Fabric is usually sold off a bolt or roll. On narrow widths the fabric is flat with a selvage at each edge, but on wider widths the fabric is folded in half lengthways so that the selvages lie together. This fold indicates where the centre of a large design or pattern should lie.

Grain

Woven fabrics are made up of two sets of threads. The crossways, or weft, threads go over and under the stronger warp threads which run the length of the fabric. The grain is the direction in which these threads have been woven. Warp threads running parallel to the selvage are on the lengthways grain. When the weft threads run perpendicular to the selvage, they are on the crossways grain.

Selvage

This is the narrow, flat band running lengthways down each side of the fabric. Here the threads are strong and closely woven, and provide a straight, ready-finished edge for seams such as the zipper opening in a cushion cover or sheer curtains.

making seams

Various seams are used in different soft furnishing projects, depending on whether the finished item needs to be strong, to withstand frequent washing or to be purely decorative.

FLAT SEAM

This is the basic seam used in most soft furnishing projects. The size of the seam allowance varies, but is usually 1.5cm/⅝in. Even if the seam will be trimmed, stitch a wider seam and trim it to get a stronger join.

1 Pin the two layers of fabric together, matching the raw edges carefully.

2 Tack (baste) 1.5cm/⅝ in in from the edge. If the fabric is fairly firm, it is possible to stitch across the pins without the need for tacking.

3 Stitch along one side of the tacking thread. Press the seam open. Zigzag-stitch or overcast the edges to prevent fraying.

FRENCH SEAM

A French seam is suitable for lightweight fabrics. It is used on bed linen to make strong seams that will not fray. The finished width of the seam can be narrower on fine fabrics.

1 Wrong sides together, stitch a 7mm/⅜in seam. Trim to 3mm/⅛ in.

2 Press the seam open. This makes it much easier to get the fold exactly on the edge at the next stage.

3 Fold, enclosing the raw edges, and press. Pin the seam and stitch 5mm/¼ in from the edge. Press to one side.

LAPPED SEAM

This seam is ideal for joining fabric that requires accurate matching as it is stitched from the right side. Plan carefully when cutting out pattern pieces in order to make the seam as inconspicuous as possible.

1 Turn under 1cm/½ in along a straight thread and press.

2 Lay the pressed edge on top of the other piece of fabric. Pin along the fold, carefully matching the design.

3 Tack (baste) the fabric if it is slippery, otherwise stitch carefully over the pins, close to the fold. For extra strength and decoration, top-stitch a further row 5mm/¼ in away.

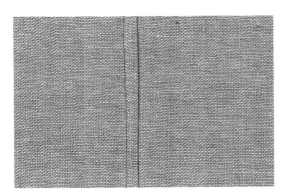

FLAT FELL SEAM

This is the traditional seam used for denim jeans. It is a strong seam that can be washed and wears well, as all the raw edges are enclosed. It is most suitable for mediumweight fabrics.

1 Pin the fabric right sides together and stitch a plain 1.5cm/⅝in seam. (For the traditional finish with two rows of stitching showing, begin with the fabric wrong sides together instead.)

2 Trim one side of the seam allowance to 3mm/⅛in. Press the wide seam allowance over the trimmed edge.

3 Turn under the edge of the larger seam allowance and pin, then tack in place. Machine stitch close to the edge of the fold.

ENCLOSED SEAMS

Seams that are enclosed (for example, inside a cushion cover) do not need to be finished, but in order to achieve a neat line when the cover is turned through they should be trimmed carefully. Bulky seams should be layered. Curved seams and corners need to be trimmed, and also snipped or notched into the seam allowance.

1 Stitch around a curved edge, using the lines on the needle plate as a guide for stitching. When you get to the corner, leave the needle in the fabric and rotate the fabric until the next seam is lined up.

2 Snip into any inward-facing points or curves to within one or two threads of the stitching. Trim the seam allowance to 5mm/¼in.

3 Cut across any outward-facing points. If the fabric is medium- or heavyweight, trim the seam allowance on either side slightly as well.

4 Notch the outward-facing curves. Cut notches closer together on tight curves, and every 2.5–5cm/1–2in on shallow curves.

5 If the seams have been stitched with multiple layers of fabric, trim them to reduce bulk. Grade the seam allowances so that the edge that is next to the right side is the largest.

preparing bias strips for piping and binding

Piping and binding add extra style to many soft furnishings projects, giving them a truly professional look and lifting them out of the ordinary.

Piping is most often used to accentuate and define the edge of shaped objects such as chair seats and cushions. Plain white piping cord is available in various widths, ready to be covered with co-ordinating fabric or a contrast fabric. Patterned fabrics look particularly

effective when one of the colours is picked out in the piping. The strips of fabric used to cover the piping cord are usually cut on the bias, but checked and striped fabrics are often cut on the straight grain to ensure that the pattern matches exactly. The covered piping cord is then sandwiched between the fabric layers of the chair seat or other item, and stitched into the seam to give a neat finish.

MAKING A BIAS STRIP

This method is suitable for small projects that require a fairly short bias strip, or where it is crucial to match a checked or striped pattern at the join.

1 Fold the fabric across at 45° so that the selvage is parallel with the straight grain running across the fabric.

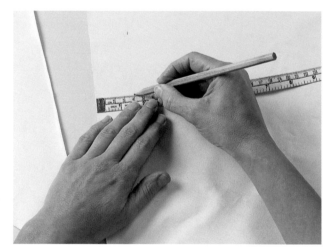

2 Press the diagonal line then open it out. Cut along this line. Decide on the width you wish the bias strip to be, and mark lines across the fabric, using a pencil and ruler. Cut sufficient strips to complete the project.

3 Join the strips by overlapping the ends at 45°. Pin, then stitch between the small triangles of fabric.

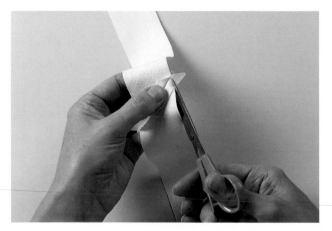

4 Press the seam open and trim off the jutting-out triangles. Join sufficient strips for the project in the same way. Steam-press the fabric to remove some of the excess stretch.

PIPING

Piping cord is available in a wide range of gauges, each of which will create a different effect. In general, the heavier-weight the fabric, the thicker the piping cord you should use. There are several different types of piping cord, the traditional cord type and the man-made kind, with a smooth outer surface that is more suitable for lightweight or sheer fabrics.

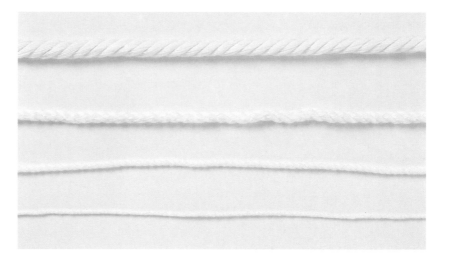

right *A range of cotton piping cords.*

Applying piping

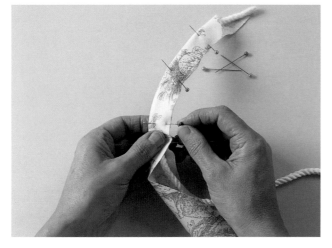

1 Cut bias strips of fabric wide enough to fit around the piping cord, leaving the required seam allowance flat. Measuring accurate seam allowances will make the piping much easier to position and stitch later on. Cut and join sufficient strips of fabric for the project (see section on preparing bias strips). Press the strips to remove some of the stretch. Fold them over the piping cord and pin in place.

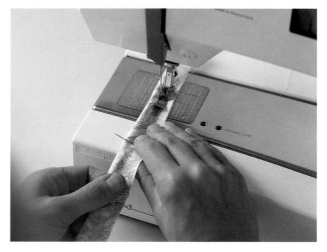

2 Fit a zipper foot to the sewing machine. Stitch as close to the piping cord as possible, removing the pins as you go. You can move the needle across slightly so that it stitches at the very edge of the zipper foot.

3 Pin and tack (baste) the piping to the edge of the main fabric. If the bias strips were cut to the correct width, the seamlines will be accurate.

4 Place the second layer of main fabric on top and pin. Tack if the fabric is slippery. Stitch as close as possible to the piping cord, moving the needle over if required.

BINDING

Binding is used to cover raw edges. It can be used to finish soft furnishings such as table linen, blinds and curtains. The width of the binding can vary from 5mm/¼in to several centimetres/inches.

Single binding

Cut strips of binding fabric on the straight grain for straight edges, or on the bias if the edge is curved. Join both straight and bias strips on the diagonal.

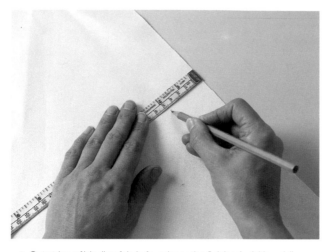

1 Cut strips of binding fabric four times the finished width, adding 3–5mm/⅛–¼ in ease, depending on the thickness of the fabric.

2 Fold over and press one-quarter of the width along one side of the binding. Fold the other side in, leaving a slight gap in the centre, and press.

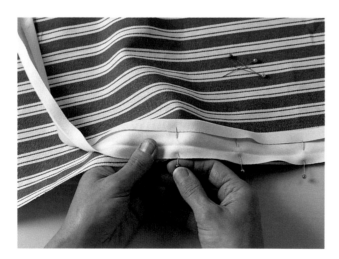

3 Open out one side of the binding and pin along the edge of the main fabric, right sides together. With deeper binding the seam allowance will be much wider than normal.

4 Stitch along the foldline, removing the pins as you reach them.

5 Fold the binding over to the reverse side and tack (baste). Hem the binding into the machine stitches. Alternatively, stitch by machine from the right side. Check that the stitching will catch the underneath edge before beginning to stitch.

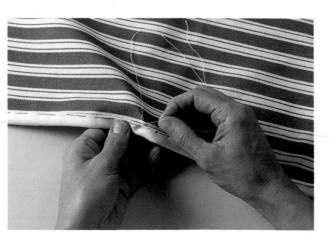

Curved edges

Cut strips of binding fabric on the bias and join as required (see section on preparing bias strips). For a large item, such as a circular tablecloth, fold the binding and press it into a similar-shaped curve to make the fitting easier. This example has a scalloped edge.

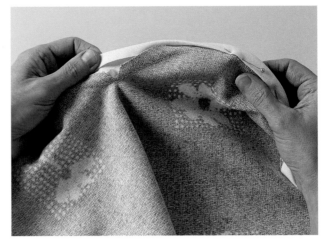

1 Fold and press the bias binding. Open out one edge and pin around the curve of the fabric. Place the pins closer together on a tight curve.

2 Stitch the binding. Keep the needle in the fabric at the point between the scallops and rotate for the next scallop. Once complete, fold the binding to the reverse side.

3 At the point between the scallops, fold the binding into a neat tuck and then pin. Hem the binding into the stitching and slip-stitch the tucks.

left *At the tuck remove the excess fabric so that the binding can lie flat on an inward facing point.*

Double binding

This quick method is more suitable for binding with lightweight or sheer fabrics. The finished binding will be stronger and less translucent.

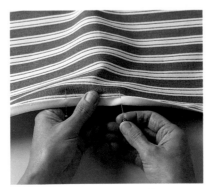

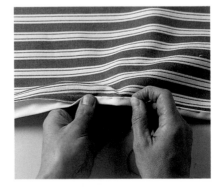

1 Cut and join bias strips of fabric six times the finished width required, adding another 3mm/⅛in for ease. Fold the strip in half and pin along the right side of the fabric.

2 Stitch along the seam allowance, which should be the same width as the finished binding. Turn the binding to the reverse side and pin.

3 Tack (baste) the binding, then hem into the stitches. Alternatively, use a machine and stitch from the right side.

buttons and buttonholes

This traditional fastening can be purely functional or a decorative part of the item. For example, buttons at the bottom of a duvet cover can be quite plain, whereas used on an envelope opening on the front of the duvet cover they will be a decorative feature. As a rule, match the buttonhole thread to the fabric rather than the button.

MEASURING THE BUTTON

1 Measure a flat button from side to side and add 3mm/⅛ in ease allowance. The allowance is so that the button will fit through the buttonhole.

2 To measure a thick or shaped button, cut a thin strip of paper and wrap it around the button. Mark with a pin and open out. Add 3mm/ ⅛ in ease.

MARKING THE BUTTONHOLE

The direction of the buttonhole depends on where any strain will be applied. The button should pull to one end of the buttonhole in the direction of the strain. If the buttonhole is stitched in the wrong direction, it could open out and the button may pop out.

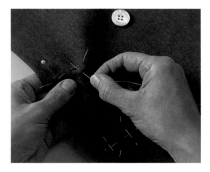

1 Mark the spacing of the buttonholes. Tack (baste) a line at each mark, along the straight grain. Mark the button length with pins, then tack. The end of the buttonhole must be at least half the length of the button away from the fold.

2 Set the sewing machine for buttonholing and fit the correct foot. Stitch the four sides of the buttonhole, changing direction exactly on the tacked lines. Finish with a few tiny straight stitches to secure the threads. Work all the buttonholes at the same time.

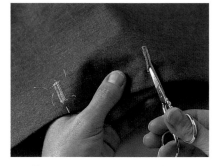

3 Remove the tacking thread. Cut along the centre of the buttonhole, using small pointed embroidery scissors or a seam ripper, taking care not to cut any stitches.

4 Line up the two sides of the openings and mark the position of the buttons with a pin. The button centre should be 3mm/⅛ in from the end of the buttonhole.

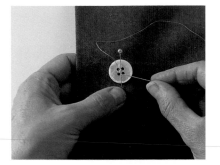

5 To make a shank, place a pin across the top of the button and stitch over the top. Remove the pin and wrap the shank with thread. Take the thread to the back and buttonhole-stitch the thread bars.

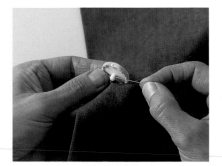

6 Covered buttons have a shank already on the underside and can be stitched straight on to the fabric.

COVERING BUTTONS

Buttons covered in the same fabric as the project look very professional. Self-covered button "blanks" are available in a range of sizes. Metal buttons are only suitable for soft furnishings that will be dry cleaned – use plastic buttons if the item will be washed. Both types of button can be used for either of the methods outlined below.

Traditional method

1 Trace or cut the appropriate-size circle from the back of the button kit packet. Cut the required number of circles out of fabric. If the buttons are loose, you will need to cut the circle 5–7mm/¼–⅜in larger than the button.

2 Tie a knot in the end of the thread. Sew a line of running stitches around the edges of the fabric circle, leaving a long tail of thread. Hold the button in the centre of the circle and pull the thread up tightly.

3 Arrange the gathers evenly and tie off. Fit the back of the button over the shank and press firmly into position. If the fabric has a pattern, check it is in the right position before fitting the back.

Using a special tool

1 Cut the circle for the button the correct size. If there is a pattern, ensure that it is centred and matches all the other buttons.

2 Lay the fabric circle on top of the appropriate hole on the base of the tool. (The sizes are marked.) Push the button down into the hole, making sure the fabric edges all face into the centre.

3 Fit the back over the shank. Position the top of the tool over the base and push down firmly. Ease the completed button out of the tool.

zippers

Zippers are one of the strongest kind of fasteners and are used for many soft furnishings. A dressweight zipper should be sufficient for most soft furnishings. There are several different ways to insert a zipper, and the method you choose will depend on its position. Fitted well, a zipper should be inconspicuous.

SEMI-CONCEALED ZIPPER

This is the easiest way to fit a zipper. It is called the semi-concealed method because the zipper teeth are visible between the folds of fabric. Use it to insert a zipper in a seam, or along the gusset of a box-style cushion.

1 Position the zipper along the edge of the opening and mark each end with a pin. Stitch the seam from the pin to the edge of the fabric at both ends.

2 Sew a row of small, even tacking (basting) stitches between the stitched seams. Press the seam open.

3 Open the zipper and place the teeth on one edge along the seam. Pin and tack 3mm/⅛ in from the outside edge of the teeth.

4 Close the zipper. Pin and tack the second side in the same way. Fit the zipper foot in the machine. Working from the right side, stitch just outside the tacking thread line. Begin partway down one side of the zipper.

5 At the corner leave the needle in the fabric and rotate, ready to stitch across the end of the zipper. Count the number of stitches into the centre and stitch the same number out the other side.

6 Remove the tacking thread from around the stitching, then snip and pull the tacking thread from the centre of the seam.

CONCEALED ZIPPER

This is a quick-and-easy way to fit a concealed zipper.

The zipper is inserted to one side of the seam so that the teeth are covered with fabric.

1 Place the pattern pieces right sides together and mark the ends of the zipper with pins. Stitch the seams from the pins to the outside edge.

2 Sew a row of small, even tacking (basting) stitches between the stitched seams. Press the seam open. Pin the zipper with the teeth in the centre of the seam. Tack 3mm/⅛ in from the teeth.

3 Close the zipper and tack the other side to match. Fit the zipper foot in the machine.

4 On the right side, stitch close to the fold on the lower edge and just outside the tacks on the upper side. Remove the tacks.

FITTING A ZIPPER BEHIND PIPING CORD

This method is often used for cushions or slipcovers

with piping. The zipper is tucked in behind the piping and is almost invisible.

1 Make the piping and tack (baste) on to the front panel of the item. Tack the zipper, face down, along the seam allowance.

2 Fit the zipper foot in the machine. Open the zipper and stitch 3mm/⅛ in away from the zipper teeth. Stitch halfway down.

3 Lift the presser foot and close the zipper, easing the slider under the foot. Stitch the rest of the way down the zipper.

4 ◁ Pin and tack the other side of the zip. Stitch 3mm/⅛ in away from the teeth, lowering the slider as before.

5 ▷ Pin and tack the seams at either end of the zipper and stitch.

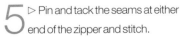

hand stitching

The majority of soft furnishings are stitched by machine, but there is often also a need for some temporary or permanent hand stitching. Temporary stitches such as tacking (basting) are used to hold fabric in position before stitching and are usually removed later. Permanent stitches include hemming and hidden stitches such as lock stitch, which is used to support curtain linings and interlinings.

TACKING (BASTING)

Work small, even tacking (basting) stitches along seams to secure before stitching. Longer, uneven tacking stitches are used to stitch substantial distances, for example, when temporarily stitching a lining before lock stitching.

SLIP TACKING (BASTING)

This is worked from the right side of the fabric. Turn over and press one seam allowance. Match the pattern along the seam and pin. Work small, even tacking (basting) stitches alternatively along the fold and then into the fabric.

RUNNING STITCH

This stitch is so called because several stitches are "run" along the needle at one time. Keep the spaces and stitches the same size. It is used for awkward seams where there is no strain.

BACK STITCH

This strong stitch is used to complete seams that would be difficult to reach by machine. Half back stitch is similar but stronger – work it in the same way as back stitch, but taking a small stitch only halfway back to the previous stitch.

HERRINGBONE STITCH

This is often thought of as an embroidery stitch but it is also useful in soft furnishings. It can be worked in small stitches instead of hemming, or as much larger stitches to hold layers of fabric together when making curtains.

index

pattern

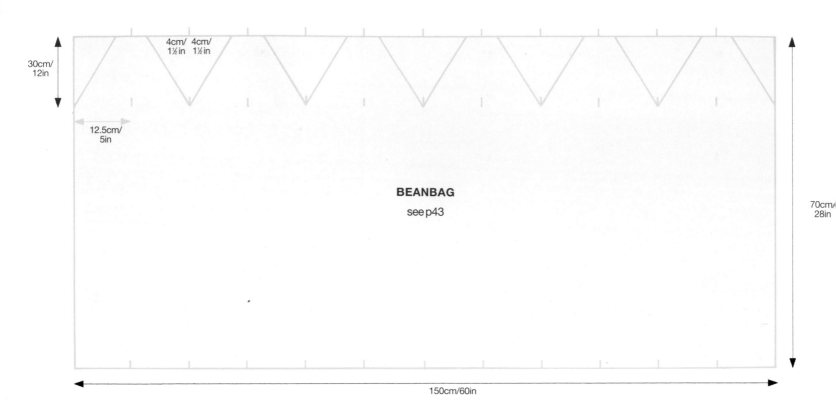

30cm/
12in

4cm/ 4cm/
1½in 1½in

12.5cm/
5in

BEANBAG

see p43

70cm/
28in

150cm/60in

acknowledgements

Berwick Street Cloth Shop, 14 Berwick Street,
London, W1V, Tel: 020 7287 2881, *for soft furnishing fabric*
Borovick Fabrics, 16 Berwick Street,
London, W1V, Tel: 020 7437 2180, *for soft furnishing fabric*
The Cloth House, 98 Berwick Street,
London, W1V, Tel: 020 7287 1555, *for soft furnishing fabric*
The Dining Chair Company, 4 St Barnabas Street,
London, SW1, Tel: 020 7259 0422, *for dining chairs, dining tables, sofas and stools*
Fabric Warehouse, Packet Boat Lane, Cowley,
Middlesex, Tel: 01895 448465, *for soft furnishing fabric*
John Lewis, 278–306 Oxford Street,
London, W1A, Tel: 020 7629 7711, *for soft furnishing fabric*
The Silk Society, 44 Berwick Street,
London, W1V, Tel: 020 7287 1881, *for soft furnishing fabric*
Thomas Dare, 341 King's Road,
London, SW3 5ES, Tel: 020 7351 7991, *for soft furnishing fabric*

**Anness Publishing Ltd and the author would like to thank the
following project makers:**
Low Wood Furnishings
Tel: 01530 222246 for the three armchair covers.
Penny Mayor for the corner pleat dining chair cover and the simple
chair cover.
Beryl Miller for the deck chair, director's chair, plastic garden chair,
scallop-edge chair, pleated chair back and two footstools.
Stewart and Sally Walton for the dish towel seat pad (p10 bottom) and the
eyelet cushion covers (p11 top)

**The publishers would like to thank the following organizations and
individuals who generously loaned images for inclusion in this book:**
Alice & Astrid p10 top right.
KA International p8 bottom, p44 bottom, p45 bottom right.
Natasha Smith p95 top.
Romo p2, p3, p8 top, p80 top, p81, p95 bottom.
Thomas Dare p10 top left.

Elizabeth Whiting Associates p56.
IPC Magazines pg 9 (Tim Imrie), p45 top (Hotze Eisma).